NICK STELLINO'S
MEDITERRANEAN FLAVORS

Nick Stellino's MEDITERRANEAN FLAVORS

Color Food Photography by E. J. Armstrong

Food Styling by Patty Wittmann

G. P. PUTNAM'S SONS
NEW YORK

G. P. Putnam's Sons
Publishers Since 1838
375 Hudson Street
New York, New York 10014

Copyright ©1997 West 175 Enterprises, Inc.
Cucina Amore is a Trademark of West 175 Enterprises, Inc.
Author Photograph by Edwin Lowe at Columbia Winery, Woodinville, WA
Front Cover Landscape Photograph by Elyse Lewin / The Image Bank
Duotone Images ©PhotoDisc, Inc., 1997
Book Design by Connie Lunde
Ceramics for Color Photography Provided by Cottura of Los Angeles

All rights reserved. This book, or parts thereof,
may not be reproduced in any form without permission.
Published simultaneously in Canada

Library of Congress Cataloging-in-Publication Data
Stellino, Nick.
Nick Stellino's Mediterranean flavors / Nick Stellino.
p. cm.
Includes index.
ISBN 0-399-14266-5 (alk. paper)
1. Cookery, Mediterranean. I. Title.
TX725.M35S74 1997   96-52935 CIP
641.59'1822—dc21

Printed in the United States of America
20 19 18 17 16 15 14 13

This book is printed on acid-free paper.

Proud Sponsors of the Cucina Amore Television Series on Public Broadcasting

I dedicate this book to Vincenzo, Massimiliana, Gladys and Sol,
whose wisdom and guidance have led me to a great adventure.

Acknowledgments

First and foremost, I would like to give thanks to my wife, Nanci, for coming up with the original idea. Without her help and inspiration, this book would not exist. I would like to thank my family - my mother, Massimiliana, my father, Vincenzo, and my brother, Mario - for their constant teachings and encouragement. I would like to share my appreciation with the whole team at West 175 Enterprises: I credit Jenny Steinle for her superb performance as my unstoppable senior food assistant; Marlene Lambert for her wonderful research; Chris Rylko for coordinating details of production and turning us all into a well-oiled machine; Pattye O'Connor for her care and attention in managing our public relations efforts; and John McLean for his role in making *Cucina Amore* known across the world.

Lastly, I owe a big debt of gratitude to my fellow dreamer, John McEwen, who remained steadfast with me to make *Cucina Amore* a reality; to Carl DeSantis for his friendship and superb legal counsel; to John Duff for the gifted and gentle editing of my stories; to E. J. Armstrong and Patty Wittmann whose photographs and food styling captured the essence of my recipes; and to Connie Lunde for her inspired book design.

Contents

Cooking From the Heart

I could not have chosen a better place in the world to be born and raised. From my decidedly prejudiced point of view, Sicily is the heart of the Mediterranean - a region abundantly rich in culture, history and culinary traditions! While I may be inordinately proud of my native country, I cannot help but marvel at the variety of foods available in an area much smaller than the United States. And the differences that distinguish the cuisines of the Mediterranean countries are as exciting as their similarities.

As unusual as many of the dishes I've presented in this book may at first appear, I have kept in mind that I want this book to be about good food that is simple to prepare using readily available ingredients without the aid of expensive kitchen machines or specialized gadgets. So, wherever possible, I have simplified the sometimes elaborate and time-consuming cooking techniques that have often been associated with the cooking from Mediterranean countries.

I have also devised recipes that, while grounded in the traditions of individual regions, do not simply duplicate the classics but capture their essence. You will be able to use familiar ingredients to create exotic-sounding dishes such as paella, moussaka, baba ghanouj or zabaglione. But these recipes are not cast in stone. I hope that they will become your culinary blueprints to create your own versions using alternative ingredients to suit your individual taste.

My greatest satisfaction will be to know that this book doesn't
sit unopened amongst your collection of cookbooks, but that it
should become dog-eared, stained with tomato sauce and olive oil,
and cluttered with your own notes from daily use.

On this journey of discovery we will experience the culinary
delights of Italy, France, Spain, Portugal, Greece and Morocco.
But, remember, no matter how good a recipe may be on the page,
it is your heart and passion that will make it sing! *Buon Appetito!*

APPETIZERS

A Trip Abroad

Smoky roasted eggplant, briny olives, fragrant sun-dried tomatoes and the ever-present garlic are fragrances shared by many of the exotic cuisines of the Mediterranean, which never fail to whet my appetite.

These aromas in particular remind me of the first time I traveled with my family from our home in Palermo, Italy, to the south of France. It was during that summer long ago that I enjoyed my first culinary experience beyond my native country. Driving through the French countryside, we came upon a charming village where we discovered a *marché alimentaire*, a wonderful little grocery store. It reminded me of the *drogherie*, the local "mom and pop" stores at home, except that the display cases were bursting with all sorts of "foreign" delicacies including *pâté de canard*, *jambon persillé*, *foie gras*, and *Camembert cheese*.

We were all like little kids in a candy store. My mom was carefully inspecting the display of pâtés while my father attacked the cheese case, inhaling the aromatic delicacies that he had never seen before. My brother was so hungry that while no one was looking, he ate the top off a baguette. The store owner clearly had a better sense of humor than our local shopkeepers because he burst into laughter and, breaking off another chunk, offered it to Mario, our hungry little urchin. Of course, choosing what to buy for our meal was the hardest part, but eventually, laden with our selection of exotic goods, we made our way to a hilltop above the village.

It was a perfect summer day. The sun warmed our faces, a gentle breeze pushed an occasional cloud across the high, blue sky. Below us, a golden carpet of wheat undulated over the hills. Mother was bursting with excitement as she got out of the car and looked upon this beautiful panorama. The look on her face was the same one that I had often seen on my brother Mario's when he walked into an ice cream store, full of wonder and anticipation.

My father came around the car and, seeing my mother, plucked a wild flower from a nearby bush. Almost in a single motion, he gallantly presented the flower to her and, drawing her close, gently kissed her. As we boys watched, enchanted by the moment, my brother whispered, "Look, Nick, it's just like they do it in the movies." My parents broke apart, laughing with a trace of embarrassment, like teenagers caught in an intimate moment.

With languid French tunes drifting from the car radio, we laid out our feast on a blanket on the ground. Without ceremony, Mario dove into the olive spread. My father cut great pieces of baguette (we had bought a whole one in addition to Mario's half-eaten loaf) with his newly acquired Opinel, a French folding knife. I was busy gulping down the pepper salami sandwiches. Mario was relishing the tangy olives and the rest of his bread. My mother sat back, the wind blowing through her hair, and drank in the landscape that she clearly found as satisfying as the food. Whether it was the place, the joy of sharing this time with my family, or the food, we had to wonder what magic had overtaken us in this foreign land.

Today, I think that we can capture at least some of the magic of that time. Begin your feast with an aromatic Onion, Pancetta and Gorgonzola Tart, or a classic Ratatouille; it may be the first step to creating your own memorable event. My wife, Nanci, often reminds me about the first time I made the Tunisian Stewed Potatoes. Its heady aroma brought neighbors to our door, asking what her *pazzo*, "crazy," husband was cooking. Now it's time to begin our culinary journey with the sounds, sights and scents of the Mediterranean. And remember, whether you're in your kitchen, or sitting on a hilltop on a sunny afternoon, as they say in France - *Laissez les bon temps rouler!* "Let the good times roll!"

If you have no idea where you want to go,
it makes little difference
how fast you travel.

ITALIAN PROVERB

Baba Ghanouj

Eggplant has always been one of my favorite childhood ingredients, so I was delighted to discover this irresistible North African eggplant dip. Don't be surprised if this addictive appetizer turns into your main course - your guests won't want to stop eating it!

1 large (1-pound) (450-g)
    eggplant

1 tablespoon olive oil

2 tablespoons roasted tahini
    (sesame seed paste)

3 tablespoons lemon juice

1 garlic clove

¾ teaspoon salt

1 tablespoon extra virgin
    olive oil

1 tablespoon chopped fresh
    Italian parsley

1 recipe Pita Bread
    (see pages 172-173),
    cut into wedges

Preheat the broiler and set the oven rack 4-6 inches (10-15 cm) from the heat source.

Wash the eggplant and prick the surface all over about 12 times with a fork. Brush with the olive oil and place on a baking sheet. Broil the eggplant, turning it approximately every 10 minutes, until the skin is charred all over and the pulp is very soft, about 30-45 minutes. As the eggplant begins to soften it will become tricky to turn. I find that holding the stem end with tongs provides me a with better grip. Remove the eggplant from the oven and cool for at least 15 minutes.

While the eggplant is cooling, place the tahini, lemon juice, garlic and salt into the bowl of a food processor or blender and process until well blended. Scrape down the sides of the bowl.

When the eggplant has cooled, cut it open with a small knife and scoop out the pulp, discarding the skin. Add the eggplant to the tahini mixture in the food processor or blender and process for 15 seconds, until smooth. (It is important to have the tahini and lemon juice mixture prepared ahead of time. Once the eggplant flesh is exposed to the air it will start to turn dark if not mixed immediately with the lemon juice.)

Spoon the Baba Ghanouj into a bowl, drizzle with the extra virgin olive oil and sprinkle with the chopped parsley. Serve with the wedges of pita bread.

Wine Suggestion - Merlot

Hummus Bi Tahini

Chickpeas are used throughout the Mediterranean, but perhaps nowhere with such universal appeal as in this traditional Lebanese spread. For the ultimate rendition, make pita bread from scratch; then sit back, and savor.

Place the chickpeas, lemon juice, tahini, water, salt, garlic, cumin and cayenne pepper in the bowl of a food processor or blender. Process for 1½-2 minutes, until smooth.

If serving immediately, spoon the hummus into a serving bowl, drizzle with the olive oil and sprinkle with the paprika and parsley. Serve with the wedges of pita bread for dipping.

If the hummus is being prepared ahead of time, cover the bowl and refrigerate for up to 1 week. (The intensity of the garlic will increase as the hummus ages.)

Wine Suggestion - Gewürztraminer

1 (15-ounce) (425-g) can chickpeas (garbanzos), drained

4 tablespoons lemon juice

4 tablespoons roasted tahini (sesame seed paste)

2 tablespoons hot water

½ teaspoon salt

2 garlic cloves

⅛ teaspoon ground cumin

⅛ teaspoon cayenne pepper

1 tablespoon extra virgin olive oil

⅛ teaspoon paprika

1 tablespoon chopped fresh Italian parsley

1 recipe Pita Bread (see pages 172-173), cut into wedges

Olive Spread

A specialty from Provence, France, known as tapenade, this hearty spread is especially appealing when you can make it up ahead of time and let the flavors mature until ready to serve. (Illustrated in this section.)

1 cup Greek or Sicilian
    black olives, pitted

3 tablespoons drained capers,
    rinsed

2 tablespoons lemon juice

1 garlic clove

1 teaspoon Dijon mustard

2 tablespoons olive oil

2 tablespoons dry Marsala
    wine

½ teaspoon black pepper

3 tablespoons drained
    water-packed tuna

In a food processor or blender, combine all the ingredients and process to form a paste. Transfer to a bowl and serve at room temperature on fresh or toasted bread slices or raw vegetables. Olive spread is also wonderful used as a garnish on grilled fish.

This spread will keep for up to a week, covered, in the refrigerator. Return to room temperature before serving.

Wine Suggestion - Merlot

Roasted Eggplant Spread on Garlic Toast

Garlic toast with toppings is Italy's way of never wasting bread - even stale bread becomes a delicacy when toasted and served with a creamy topping. Don't limit yourself to garlic toast as an appetizer, it can be a wonderful brunch, light lunch or picnic dish.

Cut the stem end from the eggplant and cut in half lengthwise. Score the flesh lightly with a sharp knife, being careful not to cut through the skin. Rub the cut surfaces with the salt and place on paper towels, cut-side-down, to drain for 20 minutes.

Preheat the oven to 425°F (220°C). Dry the cut surfaces of the eggplant halves and brush with the olive oil. Place, cut-side-down, on a nonstick baking sheet and bake for 20-30 minutes. The eggplant is completely cooked when it dents easily as you poke the skin. Remove from the oven and cool for 15 minutes.

Scoop the pulp from the eggplant halves into a colander. Place a saucer or small plate on the eggplant and place a weight on top (a large can of tomatoes works well). Drain for 20 minutes, until most of the juices have been pressed out.

Place the eggplant in a food processor or blender with all the remaining ingredients except the garlic toast and process to a smooth consistency. Serve on the garlic toast.

1 (1-pound) (450-g) eggplant

⅛ teaspoon salt

1 tablespoon olive oil

3 tablespoons freshly grated
   Pecorino Romano cheese

¼ cup Olive Spread
   (see page 14)

1 tablespoon chopped fresh
   Italian parsley

1 tablespoon lemon juice

1 recipe Toasted Garlic Bread
   (see page 229)

Cook's Tip

Add zesty tang by spreading a thin layer of goat cheese on the garlic toast before topping with the eggplant spread.

Wine Suggestion - Cabernet

Sun-dried Tomato and Cheese Spread on Garlic Toast

There is no limit to the ingredients you can use to top garlic toast. The combination of goat cheese and sun-dried tomatoes in this spread is strong and satisfying. (Illustrated in this section.)

½ cup ricotta cheese

¼ cup goat cheese

2 tablespoons chopped oil-
    packed sun-dried tomatoes

½ teaspoon salt

¼ teaspoon black pepper

½ teaspoon garlic powder

1 tablespoon lemon juice

1 tablespoon chopped
    fresh basil or
    1 teaspoon dried

1 recipe Toasted Garlic Bread
    (see page 229)

4 tablespoons freshly grated
    Parmigiano Reggiano
    cheese

Combine the ricotta cheese, goat cheese, sun-dried tomatoes, salt, pepper, garlic powder, lemon juice and basil in a small mixing bowl. Stir well to combine the ingredients completely and set aside. (The topping can be prepared the day before and refrigerated, covered, until needed.)

To serve, spread each slice of the garlic toast with the topping and sprinkle with the Parmigiano Reggiano cheese. Place on a baking sheet and broil for 2-3 minutes, until the cheese is bubbly and browned. Serve immediately.

Wine Suggestion - Sauvignon Blanc

Spanish Peppers on Garlic Toast

What's more festive: the red, green and yellow colors of the sweet bell peppers or the gay brightness from the sherry? Both ingredients combine to create a Spanish-style fiesta attitude for your guests. (Illustrated in this section.)

Heat the olive oil in a large sauté pan set on high heat until sizzling, about 2 minutes. Add all the ingredients except the sherry and the garlic toast and cook until the onions and peppers begin to brown and go limp, about 3-4 minutes. Stir in the sherry, scraping up any brown bits from the bottom of the pan. Reduce the heat to medium, cover and simmer for 4-5 minutes. Remove the lid and cook for 1-2 minutes longer, until the sherry has reduced by half, producing a thickened sauce.

The peppers are ready to be served, but will develop a fuller flavor if refrigerated overnight. Return to room temperature and serve on the garlic toast.

Cook's Tip

If you prefer a topping that is smoother, purée the cooked pepper mixture in a food processor for 30 seconds to 1 minute - the consistency will still be slightly chunky.

The puréed spread is a wonderful condiment to serve with grilled chicken breasts or fish.

Wine Suggestion - Chardonnay

5 tablespoons olive oil

4 garlic cloves, thickly sliced

½ white onion, cut lengthwise into ¼-inch (6-mm) slices

3 yellow or red bell peppers, cut in half lengthwise, then cut across in ¼-inch (6-mm) slices

1½ tablespoons anchovy paste

1 teaspoon oregano

1 teaspoon thyme

¼ teaspoon salt

¼ teaspoon black pepper

¼ teaspoon red pepper flakes

1 cup dry sherry

1½ recipes Toasted Garlic Bread (see page 229)

Artichoke Spread on Garlic Toast

↓

SERVES 6 TO 8

Using canned artichokes makes this a dish that you can toss together in a matter of minutes. I find that using artichoke hearts gives a fresher, more rustic flavor and texture. (Illustrated in this section.)

1 (13¾-ounce) (390-g) can artichoke hearts or bottoms, drained or 1 (9-ounce) (250-g) package frozen artichoke hearts, thawed, ends of leaves trimmed

3 tablespoons mayonnaise

1 garlic clove

1 tablespoon lemon juice

1 tablespoon chopped fresh Italian parsley

2 tablespoons freshly grated Parmigiano Reggiano cheese

2 tablespoons chopped prosciutto or ham

½ teaspoon salt

¼ teaspoon black pepper

1½ recipes Toasted Garlic Bread (see page 229)

Process all the ingredients except the garlic toast in a food processor or blender for 30 seconds to 1 minute, until a smooth, spreadable consistency is reached. Serve at room temperature on the garlic toast.

Cook's Tip

To serve this appetizer hot, spread the garlic toast with the artichoke topping, sprinkle with a little grated cheese of your choice and broil until golden brown and bubbly.

Wine Suggestion - Chardonnay

Mushroom Spread on Garlic Toast

Savory Swiss cheese, spiced with garlic, white wine vinegar and brandy, takes the common mushroom to new heights. An easy - and fabulous - way to start any meal.

In a large bowl, mix the mushrooms, garlic, parsley and thyme. Cover and let sit at room temperature for 2 hours to allow the flavors to marry.

Heat the olive oil in a large sauté pan set on high heat until almost smoking, about 2 minutes. Add the mushroom mixture and cook for 5-6 minutes, until all the juices have cooked away and the mushrooms begin to brown. Add the brandy, stirring to scrape up any brown bits from the bottom of the pan, and cook until it has evaporated, about 1 minute.

Transfer the mushroom mixture to a food processor and add the remaining ingredients except the garlic toast. Process for 1 minute, until you have a spreadable but slightly chunky consistency. Serve on the garlic toast.

Wine Suggestion - Cabernet-Merlot

1 pound (450 g) mushrooms, roughly chopped

4 garlic cloves, chopped

2 tablespoons chopped fresh Italian parsley

2 tablespoons chopped fresh thyme or 1 teaspoon dried

4 tablespoons olive oil

⅓ cup brandy

½ teaspoon salt

¼ teaspoon black pepper

2 tablespoons cream cheese

¼ cup shredded Swiss cheese

2 tablespoons white wine vinegar

1 recipe Toasted Garlic Bread (see page 229)

Tuna and White Bean Spread on Garlic Toast

⌄

SERVES 6 TO 8

At the last moment, a can of tuna can be your most useful ingredient. In this spread of ultra-simplicity, tuna and white beans are combined with spicy Tabasco sauce, mayonnaise, and salty capers to be ready for your lucky guests in just minutes.

1 (6-ounce) (175-g) can
   water-packed light tuna,
   drained

1 (15½-ounce) (440-g) can
   white beans, drained

2 tablespoons mayonnaise

¼ teaspoon Tabasco sauce

1 tablespoon chopped fresh
   Italian parsley

3 tablespoons drained capers,
   coarsely chopped

1 tablespoon lemon juice

Zest of ½ lemon, grated

1 recipe Toasted Garlic Bread
   (see page 229)

Process all the ingredients except the garlic toast in a food processor or blender for 30 seconds to 1 minute, until it reaches a smooth spreading consistency. Serve at room temperature on the garlic toast.

Wine Suggestion - Chenin Blanc

Chickpea Flour Fritters

In Sicily, it seems as if everyone eats these fritters known as panelle. They are available both from vendors on street corners who fry them while you wait, or neighborhood restaurants where a plate of hot, golden fritters appears on your table as the ultimate welcome.

In a large saucepan, combine the flour, water, parsley, salt, pepper and cheese, whisking to eliminate any lumps. Place the pan on medium-high heat and cook, stirring with a wooden spoon, until the mixture thickens to the consistency of polenta. After 4-5 minutes you will notice large lumps starting to appear as the mixture begins to thicken. Just continue stirring and it will smooth out to a very thick mixture. The fritter batter is ready when it begins pulling away from the sides of the pan. Remove from the heat and set aside.

Grease an 11 x 17-inch (28 x 43-cm) baking sheet and pour the batter onto it. With a wet spatula, spread the batter to the edges of the pan in an even layer. Cover the pan with a piece of oiled waxed paper and cool in the refrigerator for at least 2 hours or overnight.

Preheat the oven to 250° F (120° C). Place 4-6 inches (10-15 cm) of oil in a deep fryer or heavy deep saucepan set on medium-high heat. Heat to 350° F (180° F) - don't let the oil get any hotter than 375° F (190° C). If you don't have a candy or deep-fat-frying thermometer, drop a 1-inch (2.5-cm) cube of bread into the oil when you think it is hot enough. If it turns golden brown in 1 minute, the oil is ready.

While the oil is heating, invert the cold mixture onto a cutting board and cut into 1½- to 2-inch (4- to 5-cm) squares. Fry 4-5 squares at a time until they are golden brown, about 2-3 minutes. Drain on paper towels, sprinkle with salt to taste and keep warm in the oven while cooking the remaining squares. Serve hot, lightly sprinkled with the lemon juice, if you wish.

1¾ cups chickpea flour

2¾ cups water

2 tablespoons chopped fresh Italian parsley

¾ teaspoon salt

½ teaspoon black pepper

4 tablespoons freshly grated Pecorino Romano cheese

Canola or vegetable oil for deep frying

Juice of ½ lemon (optional)

Wine Suggestion - Semillon-Chardonnay

Cauliflower with Capers and Olives

I took the sauce from one of my favorite Italian pastas - Pasta Puttanesca - and combined the olives and capers with tender cauliflower florets. The balsamic vinegar-sugar syrup added at the end is the secret step for ultra-gloss and ultra-zest!

5 tablespoons olive oil

1 pound (450 g) cauliflower florets, cut into 1-inch (2.5-cm) chunks

1 cup pitted Greek or Sicilian black olives

¼ cup drained capers

4 garlic cloves, thickly sliced

1 tablespoon anchovy paste

¼ teaspoon red pepper flakes

2 tablespoons chopped fresh Italian parsley

½ cup Chicken Stock (see page 225)

1 cup Tomato Sauce (see page 222)

2 tablespoons balsamic vinegar

1 tablespoon sugar

1 recipe Toasted Garlic Bread (see page 229)

Heat 3 tablespoons of the olive oil in a large sauté pan set on high heat until sizzling, about 2 minutes. Add the cauliflower and cook until brown, about 3 minutes. Remove to a plate and set aside.

Add the remaining olive oil to the same pan and heat on high until sizzling, about 2 minutes. Stir in the olives, capers, garlic, anchovy paste, red pepper flakes and parsley, being careful of spattering from the oil. Cook for 1 minute, until the garlic is brown. Add the chicken stock, tomato sauce and the reserved cauliflower. Reduce the heat to medium-high and cook for 5 minutes, until the sauce thickens.

In a small saucepan set on high heat, cook the vinegar and sugar until reduced by half and quite syrupy, about 2 minutes. Stir into the cauliflower.

Transfer the cauliflower to a bowl, cover and refrigerate overnight. Serve at room temperature with garlic toast on the side.

Wine Suggestion - Gewürztraminer

Ratatouille

A more divine way to use summer-ripened zucchini, bell peppers and eggplant has yet to be devised. In its native country of France, there are innumerable variations. And don't forget - ratatouille is good the first day, and even better the second!

Sprinkle the eggplant cubes with ¼ teaspoon of the salt and place in a colander set inside a bowl to catch the juices. Cover with a small plate, place a weight on top (a large can of tomatoes works well) and drain for 15-20 minutes. Pat the eggplant dry with a towel and set aside.

Heat 3 tablespoons of the olive oil in a large nonstick sauté set on high heat until sizzling, about 2 minutes. Add the drained eggplant, cook for 5 minutes, tossing several times, then remove to a bowl.

Add the remaining olive oil to the same pan and heat on high heat until sizzling, about 2 minutes. Cook the onion, peppers and zucchini for 2 minutes, stirring occasionally. Add the garlic, red pepper flakes, thyme, oregano, parsley, pepper and the remaining salt and cook for 3 minutes, until the vegetables have browned. Pour in the vegetable or chicken stock and the browned eggplant and cook until reduced by half, about 2 minutes. Stir in the tomato sauce and cook until the sauce is thick, about 2 minutes. The vegetables may be cooled to room temperature and served, but the flavors will be more fully developed if refrigerated overnight, then returned to room temperature before serving.

Wine Suggestion - Cabernet Franc

1 (1-pound) (450-g) eggplant, cut into 1-inch (2.5-cm) cubes

¾ teaspoon salt

6 tablespoons olive oil

½ white onion, cut into 1-inch (2.5-cm) pieces

1 large red bell pepper, cut into 1-inch (2.5-cm) pieces

1 large yellow bell pepper, cut into 1-inch (2.5-cm) pieces

2 zucchini, quartered lengthwise then cut into ½-inch (1.5-cm) pieces

4 garlic cloves, thickly sliced

¼ teaspoon red pepper flakes

2 tablespoons chopped fresh thyme or 2 teaspoons dried

1 tablespoon chopped fresh oregano or 1 teaspoon dried

1 tablespoon chopped fresh Italian parsley

¼ teaspoon black pepper

½ cup Vegetable or Chicken Stock (see page 223 or 225)

¾ cup Tomato Sauce (see page 222)

Cheese-Stuffed Eggplant

↓

SERVES 8

The Japanese eggplants in this recipe are smaller than the more common "globe" variety, making them perfect for individual servings. (Illustrated on the opposite page.)

4 Japanese eggplants

½ teaspoon salt

2 tablespoons olive oil

6 tablespoons freshly grated
  Parmigiano Reggiano
  cheese

4 tablespoons goat cheese
  or ricotta cheese

¼ teaspoon black pepper

1 egg, separated

¼ cup Italian Bread Crumbs
  (see page 230)

2 tablespoons chopped oil-
  packed sun-dried tomatoes

1 head Roasted Garlic
  (see page 218)

⅔ cup Chicken Stock
  (see page 225)

Cut the eggplants in half lengthwise, leaving the stems attached. Score the flesh with a sharp knife, making sure you don't cut through the skin. Rub the cut surfaces with ¼ teaspoon of the salt. Set the eggplant halves, cut-side-down, on paper towels and drain for 15 minutes.

Preheat the oven to 400° F (200° C). Brush the cut surfaces of the eggplant halves with the olive oil and place them, cut-side-down, on an 18 x 13-inch (46 x 33-cm) nonstick baking sheet. Bake for 15 minutes. The eggplants will not cook completely through, the skin and flesh will just be softened. Cool for 30 minutes.

Gently scoop the pulp from the partially cooked eggplants, reserving the skins intact (the stem makes a good handle), and place in a food processor. Add 2 tablespoons of the Parmigiano Reggiano cheese, the goat or ricotta cheese, the remaining salt, the pepper, egg yolk, bread crumbs, sun-dried tomatoes and roasted garlic. Process just until mixed, about 30 seconds.

Preheat the oven to 425° F (220° C). Whip the egg white in a small bowl with a hand mixer until stiff. Fold into the eggplant mixture with a rubber spatula. Fill the reserved eggplant skins with the eggplant mixture, mounding it slightly. Place in a 9 x 13-inch (23 x 33-cm) baking dish and pour the chicken stock around them. (The stock may go up to the top edge of the eggplant halves, but don't worry, it evaporates quickly in the oven.) Sprinkle the stuffed eggplant halves with the remaining Parmigiano Reggiano cheese and bake for 30 minutes, until golden brown. Cool for 5-10 minutes and serve.

Wine Suggestion - Merlot

OPPOSITE: (TOP) SARDINIAN CRACKER BREAD (PAGE 171); CLOCKWISE BENEATH BREAD, OLIVE SPREAD (PAGE 14); CHEESE-STUFFED EGGPLANT (PAGE 24); SAVORY CHEESE PASTRIES (PAGE 29).

Tunisian Stewed Potatoes

SERVES 4 TO 6

Do not underestimate the power of potatoes - my neighbors walked from around the block to knock on my door and find out what I was cooking the day I made this recipe. Expect dinner guests when you make this dish.

Heat the olive oil in a large sauté pan set on high heat until sizzling, about 2 minutes. Add the potatoes and cook for 2 minutes, stirring occasionally, until they begin to brown. Stir in the onion, garlic, paprika, cardamom, cayenne, salt, pepper, parsley and basil and cook for 2-3 minutes longer. Add the chicken stock and tomato sauce, reduce the heat to medium and cover. Simmer for 3-5 minutes, until the potatoes are easily pierced with a fork. Remove the lid and cook until the sauce has thickened and reduced to a stew-like consistency, about 2 minutes.

Transfer the potatoes to a serving bowl and serve at room temperature. I think the flavor on this dish is even better if refrigerated overnight and served the next day.

Wine Suggestion - Syrah

2 tablespoons olive oil

1 pound (450 g) white potatoes, peeled and cut into ½-inch (1.5-cm) dice

1 onion, cut in half lengthwise then thinly sliced

4 garlic cloves, thickly sliced

1 teaspoon paprika

¾ teaspoon cardamom

¼ to ½ teaspoon cayenne pepper (to taste)

½ teaspoon salt

¼ teaspoon black pepper

1 tablespoon chopped fresh Italian parsley

1 tablespoon chopped fresh basil or 1 teaspoon dried

¾ cup Chicken Stock (see page 225)

¾ cup Tomato Sauce (see page 222)

OPPOSITE: MOROCCAN MELON, ORANGE AND OLIVE SALAD (PAGE 58). PREVIOUS LEFT PAGE, CLOCKWISE FROM TOP: SUN-DRIED TOMATO AND CHEESE SPREAD ON GARLIC TOAST (PAGE 16), SPANISH PEPPERS ON GARLIC TOAST (PAGE 17), ARTICHOKE SPREAD ON GARLIC TOAST (PAGE 18). PREVIOUS RIGHT PAGE, TOP: FRENCH FENNEL SOUP (PAGE 45), BOTTOM: TUNISIAN CHICKPEA SOUP (PAGE 50).

Potato Croquettes

You'll find a version of these popular potato croquettes popping up in many Mediterranean countries. Prepare them up to a day ahead of time and refrigerate until cooking. I also love them with grilled meat and fish.

2 pounds (900 g) Russet
    potatoes, peeled and
    quartered

1 head garlic, separated into
    cloves and peeled

¼ teaspoon garlic powder

¾ teaspoon salt

½ teaspoon black pepper

¾ cup freshly grated
    Pecorino Romano cheese

2 tablespoons chopped fresh
    Italian parsley

2 eggs, separated

1 whole egg

1 cup Italian Bread Crumbs
    (see page 230)

Canola or vegetable oil
    for deep frying

Put the potatoes and garlic into a large saucepan with enough cold water to cover by 2 inches (5 cm). Cover the pot and bring to a boil. Uncover, reduce the heat to medium-low and cook for 15-20 minutes, until the potatoes are so soft they will break with pressure from the back of a spoon.

Drain the potatoes and garlic, return to the pan and mash until smooth. Add the garlic powder, salt, pepper, cheese, parsley and 2 egg yolks and mix well, using a sturdy wooden spoon or electric mixer. Refrigerate for at least 2 hours, uncovered, stirring occasionally, or cover and refrigerate overnight.

Mix the whole egg with the whites from the separated eggs in a shallow bowl. Place the bread crumbs in another shallow bowl. Set both aside.

Preheat the oven to 300° F (150° C). Place 4-6 inches (10-15 cm) of the oil in a deep fryer or heavy deep saucepan set over medium heat and heat to 370° F (188° C). (Use a candy thermometer to measure the temperature. If you don't have a thermometer, heat until a sprinkle of bread crumbs dropped into the oil begins to color within seconds.)

While the oil is heating, shape 1 tablespoon measures of the mashed potatoes into football-shaped ovals. Roll each oval in the beaten egg mixture and then roll in the bread crumbs. Place on a baking sheet until ready to fry.

When the oil is hot, carefully add 4 to 5 potato ovals to the oil, cooking until golden brown, about 4-5 minutes. Using a slotted spoon, remove the croquettes to a paper towel-lined tray. Keep warm in the oven while frying the remaining croquettes. Serve immediately.

Cook's Tip

The variety of flavoring ingredients that can be added to the potato croquettes is limited only by your imagination. Here are a few of my favorites:

- Add ¾ cup very finely chopped ham to the potato mixture.

- Add 1 ounce (30 g) dried porcini mushrooms that have been softened in 1 cup hot water for 30 minutes, drained and finely chopped and 1 tablespoon chopped fresh rosemary. Omit the parsley.

- Add 3 tablespoons chopped fresh basil and 6 tablespoons chopped oil-packed sun-dried tomatoes. Omit the parsley.

Wine Suggestion - Semillon-Chardonnay

These wonderful little treats are testimonials to my mother's creativity in the kitchen. Even now when I visit home, I always ask her to make me a fresh batch.

Stuffed Romaine Leaves

In its classic rendition in Turkey and Greece, this speciality, called dolmathes, is made with grape leaves. But, not only are romaine leaves much more accessible than grape leaves, you'll be surprised by their chewy texture and almost nutty taste.

2 cups water

1 cup long-grain rice

½ cup currants

⅓ cup toasted pine nuts

⅓ cup drained capers

2 tablespoons lemon juice

2 tablespoons extra virgin
    olive oil

4 tablespoons chopped fresh
    dill or 4 teaspoons dried

¼ teaspoon salt

¼ teaspoon black pepper

1 teaspoon ground cumin

2 heads romaine lettuce

Bring the water to a boil in a medium saucepan. Stir in the rice and return to a boil. Reduce the heat to low, cover and cook for 20 minutes, until all the water has been absorbed. Transfer the rice to a large mixing bowl and add all the remaining ingredients except the romaine. Cool the filling in the refrigerator for 1 hour.

While the filling is cooling, bring a large pot of water to a boil. Fill a large bowl with ice water. Remove 10-12 leaves from each head of romaine. Use the larger leaves, not the smaller inner ones. Dip 2 leaves at a time into the hot water for no more than 10 seconds and then immediately dip them into the ice water to stop the cooking. Pat the leaves dry and then cut the bottom one-third from each leaf. You should have leaves 4-5 inches (10-13 cm) long.

Place 2 tablespoons of the chilled filling mixture down the middle of each leaf. Fold the bottom of the leaf (the edge closest to you) over the filling, then fold the sides in toward the center. Roll away from you to form a tight bundle. Place, seam-side-down, on a plate, cover and refrigerate overnight to let the flavors marry. Serve chilled or at room temperature.

Cook's Tip

The stuffing for the romaine leaves is wonderful to use on its own as a rice salad.

Wine Suggestion - Gewürztraminer

Savory Cheese Pastries

MAKES 26 TO 30 PASTRIES • SERVES 10 TO 12

Phyllo dough pastries are made in many countries that border the Mediterranean Sea. The pastries can be made several weeks ahead of time, frozen, then thawed before baking. (Illustrated in this section.)

Chop the garlic and lemon zest together until finely minced and transfer to a medium bowl. Add the feta cheese, ricotta cheese, egg, parsley, cumin, saffron or turmeric and Tabasco sauce and mix well. Set aside.

Place the phyllo dough on a flat surface and cut through the stack crosswise, making 2 equal stacks. Put the 2 stacks on top of each other and cover with a dampened paper towel.

Preheat the oven to 375° F (190° C). To assemble the pastries, take a sheet of phyllo from the stack and place it in front of you, with the short side closest to you. Lightly brush with the melted butter. Place 1 tablespoon of the cheese filling on the pastry 1 inch (2.5 cm) from the bottom in the center of the sheet. Fold the right third of the sheet to the center, covering the cheese, then fold the left third over the cheese. Bring the bottom right corner of the roll up and across to the opposite side, forming a triangle. Continue folding in this manner, as if you were folding a flag. The phyllo is fragile, so handle it carefully. Don't worry about small tears that may occur as you begin to fold, they will be folded to the inside as you continue folding. Place the finished triangle on a greased baking sheet and brush the top with the melted butter. Repeat with the remaining phyllo and filling. You should have 26-30 pastries.

Bake for 20-25 minutes, until the tops are golden brown. Let cool for about 10 minutes and serve warm.

Wine Suggestion - Semillon

4 garlic cloves

Zest of 1 lemon

¾ pound (350 g) feta cheese, crumbled

¼ cup ricotta cheese

1 egg

½ cup chopped fresh Italian parsley

½ teaspoon ground cumin

⅛ teaspoon saffron powder or turmeric

¼ teaspoon Tabasco sauce

½ pound (225 g) frozen phyllo dough, thawed

6 tablespoons melted butter

Rice Balls with Four Cheeses

↓

MAKES 24 TO 26 BALLS • SERVES 8 TO 10

A version of rice balls can be found at almost every neighborhood restaurant in Sicily. Their name in Italian, "arancine," means "little oranges," which these plump, golden globes resemble. Make them up a day ahead of time and refrigerate until ready to fry.

2 cups Chicken Stock
   (see page 225)

⅛ teaspoon saffron powder
   or turmeric

½ teaspoon salt

¼ teaspoon black pepper

1 cup short-grain rice,
   preferably arborio

2 tablespoons butter

2 tablespoons freshly grated
   Parmigiano Reggiano
   cheese

2 tablespoons freshly grated
   Asiago cheese

2 tablespoons freshly grated
   provolone cheese

24 (½-inch) (1.5-cm) cubes
   fresh or regular mozzarella
   cheese, about 2 ounces
   (60 g)

1¾ cups Italian Bread Crumbs
   (see page 230)

3 eggs, beaten

Canola or vegetable oil
   for deep frying

Bring the chicken stock, saffron or turmeric, salt and pepper to a boil in a medium saucepan set on medium-high heat. Stir in the rice and return to a boil. Reduce the heat to low and simmer, covered, for 15 minutes for short-grain pearl rice or 20 minutes for arborio rice, until the rice has absorbed the liquid. Stir in the butter, Parmigiano Reggiano, Asiago and provolone cheeses. The mixture will be thick and sticky. Let the rice cool to room temperature, then cover and refrigerate for at least 2 hours or overnight.

To assemble the rice balls, line up the ingredients in the following order: a medium bowl of cold water, the chilled rice mixture, the mozzarella cubes, a bowl with half the bread crumbs, a bowl with the beaten eggs and a bowl with the remaining bread crumbs. Moisten your hands in the bowl of water, shaking off the excess. Place 1½ tablespoons of the rice in the palm of your hand and make a deep indentation in it with your finger to form a pocket. Put a cube of mozzarella cheese into the pocket and then fold the rice over the filling. Using both hands, roll the rice into a tightly packed ball. Roll the rice ball in the first bowl of bread crumbs, dip it in the beaten eggs and then roll it in the second bowl of bread crumbs. Place on a baking sheet and repeat until you have used up all the rice. You should have approximately 24-26 balls. The rice balls can be frozen at this point and cooked later, if you wish. Simply place them on a baking sheet and freeze until firm. Transfer to re-sealable plastic bags and freeze for up to 2 months. Thaw overnight in the refrigerator before deep-frying.

Place 4-6 inches (10-15 cm) of the oil in a deep fryer or heavy deep saucepan set over medium heat and heat to 350° F (180° C). (If you don't have a candy or deep-fat-frying thermometer, drop a 1-inch (2.5-cm) cube of bread into the oil when you think it is hot enough. If it turns golden brown in 1 minute, the oil is ready.) When the oil is ready, deep-fry 2-3 rice balls at a time until golden brown, about 3-4 minutes. Drain on paper towels or brown paper bags and then keep warm in a low temperature oven while cooking the remaining rice balls. Serve hot. Any leftover cooked rice balls can be frozen for up to 2 months. Reheat the frozen rice balls on a baking sheet in a 400° F (200° C) oven for 30-40 minutes.

The rice balls may be oven-baked, if you prefer not to deep-fry them. Bake in a 400° F (200° C) oven for 20-25 minutes or 30-40 minutes for frozen rice balls, until nicely browned.

The seductive flavor of these Sicilian specialities is world renowned. All you need is to try them once and you will know what I mean.

Cook's Tip

This recipe can be modified to create one of Sicily's most famous rice recipes - Arancine di Riso con Carne (Stuffed Rice Balls with Meat Filling). Use 6 tablespoons of grated Parmigiano Reggiano cheese in place of the mixture of 3 grated cheeses used in the recipe above and ¼ cup of Bolognese Meat Sauce (see page 227) combined with ¼ cup frozen peas that have been thawed as a filling. Prepare the rice as directed, filling each ball with 1 teaspoon of the meat sauce mixture and a cube of mozzarella cheese. Cook as directed.

Wine Suggestion - Semillon

Onion, Pancetta and Gorgonzola Tart

SERVES 6 TO 8

Don't miss the perfect combination of flavors from sweet onion, bacon and tangy Gorgonzola cheese. Slivers of this tart are a lovely nibble for the beginning of a meal, but you can always serve large slices with a green salad and bread for a main course.

½ recipe Pie Dough
   (see page 232)

2 tablespoons olive oil

½ cup diced pancetta or bacon

1 cup Onion Purée
   (see page 219)

2 egg yolks

¼ cup crumbled Gorgonzola
   cheese

Line a round 8-inch (20-cm) fluted tart pan with a removable bottom with the dough and prick the bottom with a fork. Cover the tart shell with plastic wrap and refrigerate for at least 30 minutes.

Preheat the oven to 375° F (190° C). Cut a square of aluminum foil 4 inches (10 cm) larger than the diameter of the pan and line the tart shell, draping it over the edges to keep them from browning too quickly. Weight the foil down with pie weights or dried beans and bake for 15 minutes. Remove the foil and cool completely before filling.

Preheat the oven to 350° F (180° C). Heat the olive oil in a medium sauté pan set on medium-high heat until sizzling, about 2 minutes. Add the pancetta or bacon and cook until crispy brown, about 2-3 minutes. Remove with a slotted spoon and drain on paper towels. Set aside.

Mix together the onion purée and the egg yolks. Pour the filling into the partially baked tart shell and sprinkle with the cooked pancetta and crumbled cheese. With a spatula, gently push the toppings down into the filling. Bake for 35-40 minutes, until the top and crust are browned. Cool for 10-15 minutes. Serve warm or at room temperature.

Wine Suggestion - Pinot Noir

Moroccan Shrimp Pouches

MAKES 26 TO 30 PASTRIES • SERVES 10 TO 12

By the time you finish with this cookbook, I know you'll be a firm believer in the special qualities of frozen phyllo dough. In my version of this Moroccan favorite, tender phyllo pastry is stuffed with spicy shrimp and cheese - a real crowd-pleaser.

Place the olive oil, garlic and the shallots in a large sauté pan set on high heat and cook for 2 minutes. Add the shrimp, cumin, saffron or turmeric and Tabasco, and cook until the shrimp turns pink, about 3 minutes. Add the wine, stir well, and cook 1 minute, until reduced by half. Stir in the tomato sauce and cook for 2 minutes, until the liquid is thick enough to coat the shrimp. Remove from the heat and transfer the mixture to a food processor. Add the parsley and ricotta and process for 30 seconds, until the shrimp is finely chopped - the texture should not be completely smooth. Taste the mixture for salt and add if needed. Set aside.

Place the phyllo dough on a flat surface and cut through the stack crosswise, making 2 equal stacks. Put the 2 stacks on top of each other and cover with a dampened paper towel.

Preheat the oven to 375°F (190°C). To assemble the pastries, take a sheet of phyllo from the stack and place it in front of you, with the short side closest to you. Lightly brush with the melted butter. Place 1 tablespoon of the shrimp filling in the center of the sheet, 1 inch (2.5 cm) from the bottom. Fold the bottom of the phyllo over the filling and roll away from you for several turns. Fold the right third of the sheet over the filling and roll for several turns. Fold the left third of the sheet over and continue rolling the pastry until you reach the end. You should now have a cigar-shaped pastry. Place on a greased baking sheet and brush the top with the melted butter. Repeat with the remaining phyllo and filling. You should have 26-30 pastries.

Bake for 20-25 minutes, until the tops are golden brown. Let cool for 10 minutes and serve warm with the lemon wedges.

2 tablespoons olive oil

4 garlic cloves, thickly sliced

¼ cup chopped shallots

1 pound (450 g) small shrimp, preferably rock shrimp

¾ teaspoon ground cumin

⅛ teaspoon saffron powder or turmeric

¼ teaspoon Tabasco sauce

¼ cup white wine

¼ cup Tomato Sauce (see page 222)

¼ cup chopped fresh Italian parsley

¼ cup ricotta cheese

¼ teaspoon salt

½ pound (225 g) frozen phyllo dough, thawed

6 tablespoons melted butter

2 lemons, cut into wedges

Wine Suggestion - Riesling

Shrimp Fritters

Dipped in the Spicy Mayonnaise, my Shrimp Fritters will undoubtedly melt quickly, one after another, into your mouth. You often see them offered at the famous tapas bars of Spain, where nibbling appetizers has become elevated to its own distinguished meal.

SPICY MAYONNAISE

½ tablespoon drained capers
1½ tablespoons chopped fresh
   Italian parsley
3 cloves Roasted Garlic
   (see page 218)
½ teaspoon Tabasco sauce
½ cup mayonnaise

SHRIMP FRITTERS

½ pound (225 g) small peeled
   shrimp (50-60 count),
   coarsely chopped
3 tablespoons Madeira,
   brandy or sherry
½ bunch (5 or 6) green onions
   including 2 inches (5 cm)
   of the green part, thinly
   sliced
2 finely chopped garlic cloves
1 tablespoon chopped fresh
   basil or 1 teaspoon dried
1 tablespoon chopped fresh
   Italian parsley
⅛ teaspoon Tabasco sauce
10 tablespoons flour
¼ teaspoon baking powder
¼ teaspoon salt
¼ teaspoon black pepper
¾ cup cold water
½ to ¾ cup vegetable oil

For the Spicy Mayonnaise, process the capers, parsley, roasted garlic and Tabasco sauce in a food processor or blender until coarsely chopped. Add the mayonnaise and pulse until thoroughly mixed. Transfer to a bowl, cover and refrigerate until ready to use.

For the Shrimp Fritters, marinate the shrimp in the Madeira, brandy or sherry for 15 minutes in a large mixing bowl. Add the green onions, garlic, basil, parsley, Tabasco sauce, flour, baking powder, salt, pepper and ½ cup of the water. Stir, adding more of the remaining water as needed to make a creamy batter the consistency of pancake batter.

Pour the oil into a large sauté pan (the oil should be ¼ inch [6 mm] deep) set on medium-high and heat until sizzling, about 3 minutes. Drop a spoonful of the batter into the hot oil - you should be able to cook 4 at a time. Cook on both sides until brown, about 1-1½ minutes per side. Drain on paper towels, then keep warm in a low oven while cooking the remaining fritters. Serve hot with the Spicy Mayonnaise on the side.

Wine Suggestion - Riesling

According to the Spanish proverb,
four persons are wanted to make a good salad:
a spendthrift for oil,
a miser for vinegar,
a counsellor for salt,
and a madman to stir it all up.

ABRAHAM HAYWARD (1801-1884)

SOUPS and SALADS

And So They Danced

With the arrival of spring, the traditional Sunday lunch in the Stellino household became a simple, sometimes hurried affair. Hearty soups and salads were always the meals of choice for those days. The recipes were simple, yes, but what wonderful flavor! I still remember vividly the soups made of dusky wild mushrooms or rich chickpea redolent with garlic. There were also bountiful salads - Sautéed Cauliflower, my mother's tangy version of classic Greek, and Calabrian Potato.

One memorable day, Mother had experimented with a recipe for Portuguese Green Soup, which she had clipped from one of her magazines, and which I have tried faithfully to re-create for this book. We all loved her version. Even my father asked for seconds. As soon as dessert was finished, my brother, Mario, and I sprang from the table eager to get to the soccer stadium where our home team, Palermo, was playing against our loathsome rivals from Catania. We bolted from the house, leaving our parents to a much deserved quiet afternoon together.

When we arrived at the stadium, I discovered that I had left the tickets on the dresser in my room. With a resolve that is still legendary in our family, I ran the twelve long blocks home as fast as my feet could carry me to retrieve the forgotten tickets.

As I entered the front door of the house, huffing and puffing, I heard the strains of a romantic song which I recognized as a favorite of my parents, an oldie from their dating days. I quickly made my way to my room, grabbed the tickets and headed out. As I passed down the hallway, I saw that the door of the *salotto* - our living room - was ajar. My curiosity overcame my anxiety to get back to the stadium, since the salotto was almost exclusively reserved for receiving guests. I pushed the door open softly to get a glimpse at the unexpected company.

In the soft shadows of the shaded room, I saw my parents in each other's arms, gently swaying to the music. My mother, still in the yellow rubber gloves she wore for washing dishes, eyes closed, rested her head on my father's shoulder. The music played on, yet the room was as quiet as silence. For my parents, it looked as if the rest of the world had disappeared. Feeling as guilty as an uninvited guest, I quietly withdrew, closed the door behind me and tiptoed out of the house.

I don't recollect who won the soccer game that day, but whenever I think of my parents, I like to remember them the way I saw them that day - young, in love and dancing in each other's arms.

It is so curious how these memories of family and food are at times so vivid. Even today, when I see my parents - a little older, a little slower, but still very much in love - I see them dancing. And I smell the rich aromas of my mother's kitchen. While I can't promise that all of the recipes in this book will do the same for your memories, you never can tell what will happen when you cook the Portuguese Green Soup, with a little bit of love.

Gazpacho

Refreshing, beautiful, easy - no wonder this cold soup from Spain is famous around the world! It has been made for centuries in Andalucía, where every cook varies the thickness and texture to their liking. Start your own gazpacho tradition, soon!

4 Roma tomatoes, cored and roughly chopped

1 green bell pepper, roughly chopped

2 cucumbers, peeled, seeded and roughly chopped

4 cups tomato juice

¾ teaspoon Tabasco sauce

1½ teaspoons salt

¼ teaspoon white pepper

1 garlic clove, minced

¼ cup red wine vinegar

¼ cup olive oil

¼ cup dry bread crumbs

2 cups ice water

1 bunch green onions, thinly sliced

¼ cup chopped fresh Italian parsley

In a food processor or blender, coarsely chop the tomatoes, bell peppers and cucumbers in 2 or 3 batches (depending on the size of your machine) to the consistency of a salsa. Add ¾ cup of the tomato juice to each batch to help the mixture chop more evenly. Transfer the chopped vegetables to a bowl. Stir in the remaining tomato juice, the Tabasco sauce, salt, pepper, garlic, vinegar, olive oil, bread crumbs, and water. Cover and chill for at least 4 hours or overnight. Serve in chilled bowls or mugs with a sprinkle of the chopped green onions and the parsley.

Wine Suggestion - Semillon

Wild Mushroom Soup

My Sicilian childhood has given me a lifelong passion for wild mushrooms. In this soup, their hearty robust quality is deepened with the addition of rosemary and brandy. It would always be my first choice on a crisp fall or winter evening.

Heat the olive oil in a small stockpot or Dutch oven set on high heat until sizzling, about 2 minutes. Add the garlic, onion, rosemary, salt and pepper and cook for 2 minutes. Stir in all the mushrooms and continue to cook for 4-5 minutes, until the mushrooms begin to release their juices. Stir in the brandy and cook for 1-2 minutes. Add the cream and stock and bring to a boil. Reduce the heat to low and simmer, uncovered, for 15-20 minutes.

Scoop the soup into a food processor or blender and process in several batches, until smooth. Return the soup to the pot and reheat.

To serve, ladle the soup into shallow soup bowls and top with slices of the mushroom and a sprinkle of the chopped parsley.

Wine Suggestion - Pinot Noir

4 tablespoons olive oil

4 garlic cloves, chopped

1 white onion, chopped

1 tablespoon chopped fresh rosemary or 1 teaspoon dried

½ teaspoon salt

¼ teaspoon black pepper

¼ pound (115 g) white or brown button mushrooms, sliced

¼ pound (115 g) shiitake mushrooms, sliced

½ ounce (15 g) dried porcini mushrooms

½ ounce (15 g) dried chanterelle mushrooms

½ cup brandy

⅓ cup whipping cream

6 cups Vegetable or Chicken Stock (see page 223 or 225)

2 large mushroom caps, sliced ¼ inch (6 mm) thick and tossed with 1 tablespoon fresh lemon juice

4 tablespoons chopped fresh Italian parsley

Roasted Eggplant and Garlic Soup

Roasted eggplant and garlic are undoubtedly a match made in heaven. The presentation of this dish is greatly enlivened with the garnish of red peppers, pesto sauce and yogurt.

2 (1-pound) (450-g) eggplants

¼ teaspoon salt

¼ cup olive oil

4 heads Roasted Garlic
(see page 218)

1 large white onion, chopped

¼ teaspoon red pepper flakes

1 teaspoon ground cumin

¼ teaspoon cinnamon

2 tablespoons chopped
fresh mint

2 tablespoons chopped
fresh Italian parsley

6 cups Vegetable or Chicken
Stock (see page 223 or
225)

¼ cup chopped roasted
red peppers

¼ cup prepared pesto sauce

½ cup strained yogurt
(see Cook's Tip, page 52)

Cut the eggplants in half and score the cut sides, being careful not to cut through the skin. Rub the cut surfaces with the salt. Drain the eggplant halves on paper towels, cut-side-down, for 20 minutes.

Preheat the oven to 450° F (230° C). Dry the cut surfaces of the eggplants and brush them with 2 tablespoons of the olive oil. Place the eggplants, cut-side-down on the baking sheet and bake for 30 minutes. Remove from the oven and cool for at least 20 minutes.

Using a large spoon, scoop the pulp from the cooked eggplant halves into a bowl, discarding the skin. Squeeze the roasted garlic from the skins into the same bowl. Set aside.

Heat the remaining olive oil in a small stockpot or Dutch oven set on high heat until sizzling, about 2 minutes. Add the onion, red pepper flakes, cumin, cinnamon, mint and parsley and cook for 2-3 minutes, until the onion is soft. Add the reserved roasted eggplant and garlic and the vegetable or chicken stock, stirring well to mix. Bring to a boil, reduce the heat to low and simmer with the lid slightly ajar for 15-20 minutes.

Process the soup in several batches in a food processor or blender until smooth. Return to the pot and reheat.

To serve, ladle the soup into shallow soup bowls and top with the roasted peppers, pesto and yogurt.

Wine Suggestion - Merlot

French Fennel Soup

SERVES 6 TO 8

The French liqueur Pernod and Italian Sambuca are the perfect enhancers for the subtle licorice-freshness of fennel. (Illustrated in the Appetizers section.)

Cut the onion, carrot, celery, garlic and 1 of the fennel bulbs into chunks. Transfer to a food processor and process until very finely chopped, but not smooth. Set aside.

Heat the olive oil in a small stockpot or Dutch oven set on high heat until sizzling, about 2 minutes. Add the chopped vegetables, the thyme, oregano, basil, bay leaf, salt and pepper and cook for 3 minutes, until the onion is soft. Stir in the Pernod or Sambuca and cook for 45 seconds. Add the potatoes, the tomatoes and their juices and the stock and bring to a boil. Reduce the heat to low and simmer with the lid slightly ajar until the potatoes are falling apart, about 20-30 minutes.

Process the soup in several batches in a food processor or blender until smooth. Return to the pot and reheat.

Finely chop the remaining fennel bulb and the fennel leaves.

To serve, ladle the soup into shallow soup bowls and sprinkle with 1 tablespoon each of the chopped fennel bulb and leaves.

Wine Suggestion - Semillon

1 white onion

1 carrot

1 stalk celery

4 garlic cloves

2 large fennel bulbs, outer layers discarded

3 tablespoons olive oil

¾ teaspoon thyme

½ teaspoon oregano

2 tablespoons chopped fresh basil

1 bay leaf

½ teaspoon salt

¼ teaspoon black pepper

¼ cup Pernod or Sambuca

½ pound (225 g) Russet potatoes, peeled and cut into ½-inch (1.5-cm) pieces

1 (1 pound) (450 g) can peeled Italian tomatoes, chopped and juices reserved

5 cups Vegetable or Chicken Stock (see page 223 or 225)

SOUPS AND SALADS 45

Rice and Pea Soup

Comfort food time. The Stellino touch is the incredible flavor imparted by a piece of Parmigiano Reggiano cheese rind, just like my Grandmother Nonna Adele used to do.

2 tablespoons butter

1 white onion, chopped

4 garlic cloves, thickly sliced

¼ teaspoon red pepper flakes

2 tablespoons + ¼ cup chopped fresh Italian parsley

½ teaspoon salt

¼ teaspoon black pepper

2 (10-ounce) (300-g) packages frozen peas

1 (3-inch) (8-cm) piece Parmigiano Reggiano cheese rind (optional)

6 cups Vegetable or Chicken Stock (see page 223 or 225)

¾ cup short-grain rice, preferably arborio

¼ cup freshly grated Parmigiano Reggiano cheese

Melt the butter in a small stockpot or Dutch oven set on medium-high heat until sizzling, about 2 minutes. Add the onion, garlic, red pepper flakes, 2 tablespoons of the parsley, the salt and pepper and cook for 3-4 minutes, until the onions are soft. Add the frozen peas, cheese rind (if you wish) and stock and bring to a boil. Reduce the heat to low and simmer, covered, for 5 minutes.

Process half the soup in a food processor or blender until smooth. Return to the pot, stir in the rice and bring to a boil. Reduce the heat to low and simmer, covered, for 15-20 minutes, until the rice is cooked.

To serve, ladle the soup into shallow soup bowls and sprinkle with the grated cheese and the remaining chopped parsley.

Cook's Tip

If you can't find a Parmigiano Reggiano cheese rind, you might try a smoked ham hock for a similar effect.

Wine Suggestion - Sauvignon Blanc

Portuguese Green Soup

⌄

SERVES 6 TO 8

So popular in Portugal, the sausage and potato combination also makes it an international favorite. The "green" in the soup comes from the collard greens, which impart an irresistible texture. For a quick and easy dinner, this is a standout.

Heat the olive oil in a small stockpot or Dutch oven set on high heat until sizzling, about 2 minutes. Add the sausage and cook until browned, about 3 minutes. Using a slotted spoon, remove the sausage to a bowl and set aside. Add the onions, garlic, red pepper flakes, saffron or turmeric, cumin, salt and pepper to the same pan and cook on medium-high heat for 3-5 minutes, stirring occasionally, until the onions are soft. Stir in the sherry and cook for 1-2 minutes. Add the potatoes and vegetable or chicken stock and bring to a boil. Reduce the heat to low and simmer, covered, until the potatoes are falling apart, about 20-30 minutes.

In several batches, process the soup in a food processor or blender until smooth. Return to the pot and add the browned sausages and the collard greens. Simmer for 5 minutes, until the greens are soft.

To serve, ladle the soup into shallow soup bowls and sprinkle with the chopped peppers.

Wine Suggestion - Chenin Blanc

2 tablespoons olive oil

1½ pounds (700 g) hot Italian sausage or chorizo, cut into ½-inch (1.5-cm) pieces

2 white onions, chopped

10 whole garlic cloves

¼ teaspoon red pepper flakes

⅛ teaspoon saffron powder or turmeric

1½ teaspoons ground cumin

½ teaspoon salt

¼ teaspoon black pepper

½ cup dry sherry

1 pound (450 g) Russet potatoes, peeled and cut into ½-inch (1.5-cm) pieces

6 cups Vegetable or Chicken Stock (see page 223 or 225)

4 cups chopped collard greens or kale

4 tablespoons chopped roasted red pepper

Almond, Onion and Orange Soup

Such an elegant golden-yellow soup! It's modeled loosely after the cold soup made with fresh ground almonds, garlic and grapes in Spain. Of course, the candied almonds sprinkled on the top are a result of my Sicilian love of sweet finishes.

ALMOND, ONION AND ORANGE SOUP

2 tablespoons butter

2 tablespoons olive oil

3 onions, chopped

4 whole garlic cloves

1½ cups chopped almonds

⅛ teaspoon saffron powder
    or turmeric

1 teaspoon ground coriander

1½ teaspoons ground cumin

2 tablespoons chopped fresh
    Italian parsley

¾ teaspoon salt

¼ teaspoon black pepper

¼ cup orange liqueur,
    such as Triple Sec
    or Grand Marnier

¼ cup fresh orange juice

½ cup whipping cream

6 cups Chicken Stock
    (see page 225)

CANDIED ALMONDS

½ tablespoon butter

1 tablespoon sugar

⅛ teaspoon salt

½ cup sliced almonds

Zest of 2 oranges, grated

For the Almond, Onion and Orange Soup, melt the butter and olive oil in a small stockpot or Dutch oven set on medium-high heat until sizzling, about 2 minutes. Add the onions, garlic, almonds, saffron or turmeric, coriander, cumin, parsley, salt and pepper and cook for 5-7 minutes, until the onion is soft. Stir in the orange liqueur and orange juice and cook for 1 minute. Add the cream and stock and bring to a boil. Reduce the heat to low and simmer, uncovered, for 20-30 minutes.

In several batches, process the soup in a food processor or blender until smooth. Return the soup to the pot to reheat.

For the Candied Almonds, melt the butter and sugar in a small sauté pan set on medium-high heat. Add the salt, almonds and orange zest and cook, stirring constantly, until glazed and caramelized, about 1-2 minutes. Transfer to a bowl immediately, so the almonds aren't burned from the heat remaining in the pan.

To serve, ladle the soup into shallow soup bowls and sprinkle with the candied almonds.

Wine Suggestion - Chardonnay

Poor Man's Chickpea Soup

Here's another standout recipe. Although the ingredients are common and humble, my guests always ask for "one more bowl," until every drop is gone. Very easy to accomplish, it's a dinner filled with flavor.

Cut the carrot, onion and celery into chunks. Transfer to a food processor, add the garlic, then process until finely chopped, but not smooth. Set aside.

Heat the olive oil in a small stockpot or Dutch oven set on high heat until sizzling, about 2 minutes. Add the chopped vegetables, red pepper flakes, bay leaf, rosemary, thyme and pepper and cook for 3-4 minutes, until the onion is soft and translucent. Add the chickpeas, ham hock, Parmigiano Reggiano rind, if you wish, chicken stock and tomato sauce and bring to a boil. Reduce the heat to low and simmer, covered, for 1 hour. (If using canned beans, simmer, covered, for 30 minutes.)

Remove the ham hock, pull the meat from the bone and cut into ½-inch (1.5-cm) pieces. Set aside.

Discard the bay leaf and rosemary. Process half the soup in a food processor or blender until smooth. Return to the pot and add the reserved ham and the arugula. Stir well.

To serve, ladle the soup into shallow soup bowls and sprinkle with the chopped parsley and the cheese.

Wine Suggestion - Pinot Gris

1 carrot
1 white onion
1 stalk celery
4 garlic cloves
3 tablespoons olive oil
¼ teaspoon red pepper flakes
1 bay leaf
1 (2-inch) (5-cm) sprig fresh
     rosemary
1 teaspoon thyme
¼ teaspoon black pepper
1½ cups dried chickpeas
     (garbanzo beans), soaked
     overnight in water and
     drained or 3 (16-ounce)
     (450-g) cans chickpeas,
     rinsed and drained
1 smoked ham hock
1 (3-inch) (8-cm) piece
     Parmigiano Reggiano
     cheese rind (optional)
5 cups Chicken Stock
     (see page 225)
1 cup Tomato Sauce
     (see page 222)
8 ounces (225-g) arugula
     or mustard greens,
     stems removed, chopped
     to yield 2 cups
4 tablespoons chopped fresh
     Italian parsley
4 tablespoons freshly grated
     Parmigiano Reggiano
     cheese

Tunisian Chickpea Soup

A very different chickpea soup, dressed up with the addition of cumin, lemon juice and feta cheese. The roasted red peppers are a perfect complement to the pale yellow color and also give a smoky roasted bite. (Illustrated in the Appetizers section.)

1 onion

1 carrot

1 stalk celery

5 garlic cloves

3 tablespoons olive oil

¼ teaspoon red pepper flakes

1 tablespoon ground cumin

⅛ teaspoon saffron powder
   or turmeric

1 teaspoon salt

½ teaspoon black pepper

1¾ cups dried chickpeas
   (garbanzo beans), soaked
   in water overnight and
   drained or 4 (16-ounce)
   (450-g) cans chickpeas,
   rinsed and drained

6 cups Vegetable or Chicken
   Stock (see page 223 or
   225)

3 tablespoons chopped
   fresh mint

3 tablespoons chopped fresh
   basil or 1 tablespoon dried

3 tablespoons lemon juice

¾ cup crumbled feta cheese

¼ cup chopped roasted
   red bell peppers

Cut the onion, carrot and celery into chunks. Transfer to a food processor, add the garlic, and process until finely chopped, but not smooth. Set aside.

Heat the olive oil in a small stockpot or Dutch oven set on high heat until sizzling, about 2 minutes. Add the finely chopped vegetables, red pepper flakes, cumin, saffron or turmeric, salt and pepper and cook for 3 minutes, until the onion is soft. Stir in the chickpeas and stock and bring to a boil. Reduce the heat to low and simmer, covered, for 1 hour. (If using canned beans, simmer, covered, for 30 minutes.)

Process half the soup in a food processor or blender until smooth. Return to the pot and add the mint, basil and lemon juice.

Serve the soup sprinkled with the feta cheese and roasted red peppers.

Wine Suggestion - Riesling

Cabbage and Sausage Soup

As you would expect, this cabbage and sausage combination will make you feel comforted and at home. But always be prepared for the unexpected Stellino touch: a dash of sun-dried tomatoes and the perfect finish of garlic toast at the bottom of your bowl.

Heat the olive oil in a small stockpot or Dutch oven set on high heat until sizzling, about 2 minutes. Add the sausage and cook for 3 minutes. Using a slotted spoon, remove the sausage to a bowl and set aside. Add the onions, garlic, red pepper flakes, salt, pepper and sun-dried tomatoes to the same pan and cook on medium-high heat for 3-5 minutes, stirring occasionally, until the onions are soft. Stir in the wine and cook for 1-2 minutes. Add the cabbage, the reserved cooked sausage and the chicken stock and bring to a boil. Reduce the heat to low and simmer with the lid slightly ajar for 10-15 minutes, until the cabbage is tender.

To serve, place a piece of the garlic toast in the bottom of a shallow soup bowl and ladle the soup over the top.

Wine Suggestion - Lemberger

2 tablespoons olive oil

1½ pounds (700 g) hot Italian sausage or chorizo, cut into ½-inch (1.5-cm) pieces

2 white onions, sliced

4 garlic cloves, thickly sliced

¼ teaspoon red pepper flakes

½ teaspoon salt

¼ teaspoon black pepper

½ cup chopped oil-packed sun-dried tomatoes

½ cup white wine

½ pound (225 g) green cabbage, thinly sliced (about 4 cups)

6 cups Chicken Stock (see page 225)

6 to 8 slices Toasted Garlic Bread (see page 229), cut ½ inch (1.5-cm) thick

Lamb and Lentil Soup

⌄

SERVES 6 TO 8

You can't go wrong with the flavor and texture contrasts of lamb, lentil and mint - humble ingredients that rise to new heights together. It's garnished with a traditional Middle Eastern tang of creamy white yogurt - you'll lap up every spoonful.

2 tablespoons olive oil

1 pound (450 g) ground lamb
   or lamb sausage, if
   available, removed
   from the casing

1 onion, sliced

4 garlic cloves, thickly sliced

¼ teaspoon red pepper flakes

1½ teaspoons ground cumin

¼ teaspoon cinnamon

7 tablespoons chopped
   fresh mint

½ teaspoon salt

¼ teaspoon black pepper

½ cup brandy

1¼ cups dried lentils, picked
   through and rinsed

6 cups Chicken or Beef Stock
   (see page 225 or 226)

½ cup strained yogurt
   (see Cook's Tip)

Heat the oil in a small stockpot or Dutch oven set on high heat until sizzling, about 2 minutes. Add the lamb to the pan and break it up with the back of a wooden spoon. Cook the lamb until browned, about 3 minutes. Using a slotted spoon, remove the lamb to a bowl and set aside.

Add the onion, garlic, red pepper flakes, cumin, cinnamon, 3 tablespoons of the mint, the salt and pepper to the same pan and cook for 3 minutes, stirring occasionally, until the onion is soft. Stir in the brandy and cook for 1-2 minutes. Add the lentils and stock and bring to a boil. Reduce the heat to low and simmer, covered, for 20-30 minutes, until the lentils are soft.

Process half the soup in a food processor or blender until smooth. Return to the pan, stir in the browned lamb and cook for 5 minutes.

To serve, ladle the soup into shallow soup bowls and top with the yogurt and the remaining chopped mint.

Cook's Tip

Strained yogurt is a creamy topping that adds wonderful flavor to soups. To make strained yogurt, place 1 cup plain yogurt in a yogurt strainer, a mesh strainer that has been lined with paper towels or a coffee filter. Set the strainer over a bowl, cover and drain in the refrigerator for 5 hours or overnight.

Wine Suggestion - Cabernet Sauvignon

French Lentil Soup

A rich, earthy soup which generated a lot of discussion from my research tests, simply because of its secret ingredient: chicken livers. I urge you to overcome any prejudices and try this for yourself - you'll be sprinkling chicken liver in many more dishes, I'm sure.

Melt the butter in a small stockpot or Dutch oven set on medium-high heat. Add the onion, carrot, celery, garlic, rosemary, bay leaf, salt and pepper and cook for 4-5 minutes, until the onions are soft. Add the livers and cook for 2-3 minutes. Pour in the brandy and cook for 1-2 minutes, stirring to scrape up any brown bits from the bottom of the pan. Stir in the cream, chicken stock and lentils and bring to a boil. Reduce the heat to low and simmer with the lid slightly ajar for 20-30 minutes, until the lentils are soft.

Process half the soup in a food processor or blender until smooth. Return to the pot to reheat.

To serve, ladle the soup into shallow soup bowls and sprinkle with the chopped parsley.

Wine Suggestion - Cabernet Franc

3 tablespoons butter

1 onion, chopped

1 carrot, chopped

1 stalk celery, chopped

4 garlic cloves, thickly sliced

2 tablespoons chopped
 fresh rosemary

1 bay leaf

½ teaspoon salt

¼ teaspoon black pepper

¼ pound (115 g) chicken
 livers, finely chopped

½ cup brandy

⅓ cup whipping cream

6 cups Chicken Stock
 (see page 225)

1 cup dried lentils,
 picked over and rinsed

4 tablespoons chopped fresh
 Italian parsley

Sicilian Fish Soup

When I make this dish at home, my guests tell me they love this fish soup more than any other! Get the freshest seafood you can find and plan on making it for an impressive special occasion. Your efforts will be amply rewarded.

3 tablespoons olive oil

1 onion, chopped

6 garlic cloves, thickly sliced

¼ teaspoon red pepper flakes

¾ teaspoon curry powder

1 cup white wine

2 cups Tomato Sauce
   (see page 222)

3 cups clam juice

4 tablespoons chopped fresh
   Italian parsley

½ teaspoon salt

½ pound (225 g) halibut fillet,
   skin removed, cut into
   chunks (see Cook's Tip)

8 Manilla clams

8 mussels, bearded and
   cleaned

8 sea scallops

8 large shrimp (13-15 count),
   peeled and deveined
   (see Cook's Tip)

4 slices thick Toasted Garlic
   Bread (see page 229)

Extra virgin olive oil
   for garnish

Heat the olive oil in a medium stockpot set on medium-high heat until sizzling, about 2 minutes. Add the onion, garlic, red pepper flakes and curry powder and cook for 3 minutes, until the onion begins to soften. Stir in the wine and cook for 3 minutes, or until reduced by half. Add the tomato sauce, clam juice, 2 tablespoons of the parsley and the salt. Bring to a boil and cook for 5 minutes.

Reduce the heat to medium, add the halibut and cook for 1 minute. (Timing is critical when adding all the seafood - you don't want to overcook it!) Add the clams and mussels and cook for 2 minutes. Remove the stockpot from the heat, add the scallops and shrimp, cover and let sit for 2 minutes.

Place a piece of the garlic toast in the bottom of each soup bowl and top with some of each of the different seafood and the broth. Sprinkle with the remaining chopped parsley and drizzle with the extra virgin olive oil. Serve immediately.

Cook's Tip

For a more flavorful soup base, simmer the clam juice with the shrimp shells and the fish skin for 15-20 minutes on medium heat. Strain and add more clam juice if necessary to bring it back to 3 cups.

Wine Suggestion - Pinot Gris

Mushroom Salad

There is no better tool for a busy cook than an easy dish you can make several days ahead and have waiting to whisk out at the final moment. The best part is that this dish only gets better the longer it marinates. Just bring it to room temperature before serving.

Heat the olive oil in a large sauté pan set on high heat until it sizzles, 2 minutes. Add the mushrooms and cook for 2 minutes, until they begin to brown. Stir in the white wine, cover the pan and cook for 2 minutes. Remove the cover and cook until the liquid has reduced by half, about 2 minutes. Transfer the mushrooms and their juices to a bowl and stir in the garlic, parsley, thyme, lemon juice, salt and pepper. Cool to room temperature or serve warm. Just before serving, stir in the extra virgin olive oil, if you wish. Top each serving with the shavings of Parmigiano Reggiano cheese.

Wine Suggestion - Pinot Noir

4 tablespoons olive oil

1¼ pounds (560 g) mixed fresh mushrooms (white button, cremini, shiitake; whatever you have available), stemmed and quartered

½ cup white wine

1 garlic clove, finely chopped

1 tablespoon chopped fresh Italian parsley

1 tablespoon chopped fresh thyme or 1 teaspoon dried

2 tablespoons lemon juice

½ teaspoon salt

¼ teaspoon black pepper

1 tablespoon extra virgin olive oil (optional)

¼ cup shaved Parmigiano Reggiano cheese

Sautéed Cauliflower Salad

Tender white cauliflower marinated in white wine is given extra zest from the anchovy paste. Anchovies, fresh, dried, and ground, have added zing to Mediterranean cooking since the dawn of culinary time - a new treasure to have on hand in your kitchen cupboard.

4 tablespoons olive oil

1 pound (450 g) cauliflower florets, cut into 2-inch (5-cm) pieces

¼ teaspoon red pepper flakes

½ cup white wine

1 garlic clove, finely chopped

2 tablespoons chopped fresh Italian parsley

2 tablespoons drained capers

½ cup pitted green olives, coarsely chopped

1 teaspoon anchovy paste

2 tablespoons extra virgin olive oil

3 tablespoons red wine vinegar

Heat the olive oil in a large sauté pan set on high heat until it sizzles, about 2 minutes. Add the cauliflower and red pepper flakes and cook for 3-4 minutes, until most of the pieces are brown on the edges. Stir in the wine, cover and cook for 2 minutes, until most of the liquid is absorbed. Transfer to a bowl and add the garlic, parsley, capers and olives.

In a small bowl, whisk the anchovy paste with the olive oil and vinegar. Pour the vinaigrette over the cauliflower and mix well. Serve warm or at room temperature.

This dish can be prepared up to 2 days ahead of time. Remove from the refrigerator 2-3 hours before serving or warm to room temperature in the microwave oven for a few minutes.

Wine Suggestion - Gewürztraminer

Roasted Pear Salad

I can't describe the enhancement that occurs when you roast pears: it's a deepening of the pears' sweetness that you simply must taste for yourself - not to mention the textural delight of a sprinkling of walnuts, Gorgonzola cheese and prosciutto ham.

Preheat the oven to 500° F (260° C). In a large bowl, mix the melted butter, honey and cinnamon. Add the pears and toss well. Spread the pear mixture on a baking sheet and roast in the oven for 20 minutes, tossing them once, halfway through.

In the same bowl, combine the sherry, vinegar, oil and black pepper. Add the roasted pears and stir to coat completely with the vinaigrette. The recipe can be prepared to this point 1-2 days ahead of time. Simply cover and refrigerate. Remove from the refrigerator 2-3 hours before you plan to serve the salad. For a warm salad, heat the pears in the microwave for 1-2 minutes.

The salad can be prepared while the pears are still warm or after they've cooled to room temperature. To assemble, place a bed of the arugula on each serving plate and top with the pears. Sprinkle with the walnuts, Gorgonzola and prosciutto, drizzle with any of the remaining vinaigrette and serve.

Wine Suggestion - Cabernet Sauvignon

1 tablespoon butter, melted

1 tablespoon honey

⅛ teaspoon cinnamon

4 firm pears, preferably Bosc, peeled, cored and cut into 1-inch (2.5-cm) pieces

2 tablespoons dry sherry

2 tablespoons white wine vinegar

1 tablespoon light olive oil or vegetable oil

⅛ teaspoon black pepper

4-5 ounces (115-150 g) arugula or baby salad greens

⅓ cup chopped walnuts, toasted

⅓ cup crumbled Gorgonzola cheese

⅓ cup prosciutto, cut into matchsticks

Moroccan Melon, Orange and Olive Salad

A picture-perfect color mixture: mint-green honeydew, juicy bright oranges, and black olives. There is no quicker way to bring the bright mood of a Moroccan moment into a drab day than this easy salad. (Illustrated in the Appetizers section.)

½ honeydew melon, peeled,
    seeded and cut into 1-inch
    (2.5-cm) pieces

4 oranges, peeled, sliced into
    ½-inch (1.5-cm) rounds
    and cut into quarters

18 large pitted California
    black olives, quartered
    lengthwise

1 tablespoon chopped
    fresh mint

¼ teaspoon cayenne

½ teaspoon cinnamon

1 tablespoon olive oil
    or vegetable oil

2 tablespoons balsamic vinegar

¾ teaspoon freshly ground
    black pepper

Place the fruit and olives in large bowl. In a small bowl, whisk together the remaining ingredients, add to the fruit and olives and toss well. Cover and refrigerate for 1 hour. Serve chilled or at room temperature.

Wine Suggestion - Riesling

Greek Salad

Enjoy this version of Greek salad on a rainy day, and with each bite let your imagination travel around the crystal clear waters of the Mediterranean Sea and the whitewashed beaches of the fabulous Greek Islands.

Place the cucumber into a colander and sprinkle with the salt. Let drain for 20 minutes and then rinse. Combine the cucumber, capers, olives, romaine lettuce, tomatoes, onion, bell pepper and feta cheese in a large bowl. In a small bowl, whisk together the anchovy paste, garlic, olive oil, vinegar, black pepper, oregano, parsley and basil. Pour over the salad and toss well. Spoon the salad onto serving dishes and place 2 wedges of the hard-cooked eggs on each side.

Wine Suggestion - Sauvignon Blanc

1 cucumber, peeled and cut
   into 1-inch (2.5-cm) pieces
⅛ teaspoon salt
¼ cup drained capers
1 cup Greek or Sicilian black
   olives, pitted and halved
1 head romaine lettuce,
   outer leaves removed,
   cut crosswise into 2-inch
   (5-cm) pieces and washed
2 Roma tomatoes,
   quartered lengthwise
½ red onion, thinly sliced,
   soaked in 1 cup cold water
   and 2 tablespoons
   white wine vinegar for
   30 minutes, drained
   and patted dry
1 green or red bell pepper, cut
   into 1-inch (2.5-cm) pieces
½ cup crumbled feta cheese
1 teaspoon anchovy paste
1 garlic clove, finely chopped
¼ cup extra virgin olive oil
3 tablespoons red wine vinegar
½ teaspoon black pepper
1 teaspoon oregano
2 tablespoons chopped fresh
   Italian parsley
2 tablespoons chopped fresh
   basil or 2 teaspoons dried
4 hard-cooked eggs, peeled
   and quartered lengthwise

Greek Salad with Tuna

My gift for creating inventive recipes with a common can of tuna came from my mother, who always had some in her cupboard. Served with a thick piece of garlic toast, this salad is a complete and satisfying meal.

1 (6-ounce) (175-g) can
    water-packed tuna,
    drained and flaked

1 pound (450 g) Roma
    tomatoes, cut into quarters
    and seeded

½ onion, thinly sliced, soaked
    in 1 cup cold water and
    2 tablespoons white wine
    vinegar for 30 minutes,
    drained and patted dry

½ cup Greek or Sicilian black
    olives, pitted and quartered

2 tablespoons drained capers +
    2 tablespoons caper liquid

4 tablespoons extra virgin
    olive oil

2 tablespoons chopped fresh
    basil or 2 teaspoons dried

2 garlic cloves, chopped

1 tablespoon chopped fresh
    Italian parsley

1 teaspoon oregano

½ teaspoon black pepper

¾ cup crumbled feta cheese

4-5 ounces (115-150 g)
    mixed baby salad greens

1 recipe Toasted Garlic Bread
    (see page 229)

Toss all the ingredients except the salad greens and garlic toast together in a large bowl and marinate for at least 30 minutes. Place the salad greens on individual salad plates and top with the salad mixture. Serve with a thick slice of the garlic toast.

Wine Suggestion - Gewürztraminer

Tabbouleh

Originally from Turkey, this is one of those dishes that has so many appealing qualities, it has found acceptance around the world. Its base, sweet crunchy bulgur wheat, is perhaps the simplest grain to prepare. So what are you waiting for - try it for yourself!

Place the bulgur in a fine mesh strainer, rinse under cold water and drain well. (There is no need to soak the bulgur in the water. It will soften as it soaks in the dressing.) Transfer to a large bowl and toss with the mint, parsley, green onions, tomatoes and cucumber.

In a small bowl, whisk together the olive oil, lemon juice, salt, pepper, cinnamon and nutmeg. Pour the dressing over the bulgur and mix well. Let the salad sit for at least 15 minutes at room temperature for the flavors to marry before serving.

Cook's Tip

This salad can be prepared a day ahead of time. Simply layer the ingredients in a bowl in the following order: bulgur, parsley, mint, onions, tomatoes and cucumber. Cover tightly and refrigerate. When ready to serve, toss the bulgur and vegetables with the dressing. Let sit for 15 minutes and it's ready to serve.

Wine Suggestion - Riesling

¾ cup fine bulgur

1 cup finely chopped
   fresh mint

4 cups finely chopped fresh
   Italian parsley (approximately 2 large bunches)

1 bunch green onions with
   green ends, finely chopped

3 Roma tomatoes, cut into
   ½-inch (1.5-cm) dice

1 cucumber, peeled, seeded
   and cut into ½-inch
   (1.5-cm) dice, 2 cups

½ cup extra virgin olive oil

½ cup lemon juice

1 teaspoon salt

¾ teaspoon black pepper

½ teaspoon cinnamon

½ teaspoon nutmeg

French Lentil Salad

A short cooking time for the lentils gives you the perfect, slightly crunchy texture, for this delightful salad. It's of French inspiration, bien sûr - time to pull out your berets?

1½ cups brown lentils,
   rinsed and drained

½ cup diced or chopped bacon

1 carrot, cut into ¼-inch
   (6-mm) dice

1 stalk celery, cut into ¼-inch
   (6-mm) dice

½ cup chopped shallots
   or white onion

3 Roma tomatoes, cut into
   ½-inch (1.5-cm) chunks

2 tablespoons chopped fresh
   Italian parsley

2 tablespoons chopped fresh
   basil or 2 teaspoons dried

½ cup crumbled Gorgonzola
   or blue cheese

¼ cup red wine vinegar

¼ cup extra virgin olive oil

½ teaspoon salt

¼ teaspoon black pepper

Place the lentils and 3 cups of cold water in a medium saucepan set on high heat. Bring to a boil, reduce the heat to medium, and cook for 20 minutes. Drain and place in a large bowl.

In a large sauté pan set on medium-high heat, cook the bacon until lightly crisped. Remove the bacon with a slotted spoon to the bowl of lentils. Reserve the bacon grease in the pan, adding enough olive oil to make 2 tablespoons. Add the carrot, celery and shallots or onion to the pan and cook over medium-high heat for 3-5 minutes, until lightly browned. Transfer the cooked vegetables to the bowl with the lentils and add the remaining ingredients, tossing well to coat. Cover and refrigerate for 1 hour to let the flavors marry. Serve at room temperature.

Wine Suggestion - Syrah

Chickpea and Tuna Salad

The fresh Lemon Vinaigrette spiked with warm Tabasco sauce just takes a minute to whisk together. Sprinkle it over a can of chickpeas and a can of tuna and it could easily become your favorite fast food.

For the Lemon Vinaigrette, combine all the ingredients in a small bowl and whisk well.

For the Chickpea and Tuna Salad, place the ingredients in a large bowl, pour over the vinaigrette and toss to combine. Cover the salad and refrigerate for 1 hour. Bring to room temperature before serving.

Wine Suggestion - Semillon-Chardonnay

LEMON VINAIGRETTE

4 tablespoons extra virgin olive oil

4 tablespoons lemon juice

¼ teaspoon Tabasco sauce

½ teaspoon sugar

¼ teaspoon salt

¼ teaspoon black pepper

CHICKPEA AND TUNA SALAD

1 (6-ounce) (175-g) can water-packed tuna, drained and flaked

2 (15-ounce) (425-g) cans chickpeas (garbanzo beans), rinsed and drained

1 red bell pepper, cut into ½-inch (1.5-cm) dice

½ red onion, peeled, halved and thinly sliced, soaked in 1 cup cold water and 2 tablespoons white wine vinegar for 30 minutes, drained and patted dry

¼ cup chopped fresh Italian parsley

2 teaspoons grated lemon zest

½ cup shaved Parmigiano Reggiano cheese (optional)

Calabrian Potato Salad

A simple potato salad from Italy, brightened with the Mediterranean tastes of rosemary, capers and olives. Your biggest surprise might come from the flavor in the humblest ingredient: the addition of the leftover potato peels.

1½ pounds (700 g) white new potatoes, washed

1 (5¾-ounce) (163-g) can large pitted California black olives, halved

1 red or green bell pepper, cut into ½-inch (1.5-cm) dice

4 tablespoons drained capers

1 garlic clove

1 tablespoon chopped fresh Italian parsley

1 tablespoon chopped fresh thyme or 1 teaspoon dried

1 tablespoon chopped fresh rosemary or 1 teaspoon dried

2 tablespoons extra virgin olive oil

2 tablespoons red wine vinegar

¼ cup mayonnaise

2 tablespoons coarsely ground mustard

½ teaspoon salt

¼ teaspoon black pepper

¼ cup potato cooking water (see directions)

Reserved potato peels (see directions)

Put the potatoes in a large pot with enough cold water to cover by 2 inches (5 cm), cover and bring to a boil. Once the water reaches a boil, remove the cover, reduce the heat to medium-low and cook for 35-40 minutes, until a knife can be inserted into the center with ease. Drain the water, reserving ¼ cup for the dressing. Cool the potatoes in their skins for an hour. Peel the potatoes by gently scraping the skin off with a sharp knife. Reserve the potato skins for the dressing. Cut the potatoes into 1-inch (2.5-cm) dice and put in a large bowl with the olives, bell pepper and 2 tablespoons of the capers.

Place the garlic, parsley, thyme, rosemary, olive oil, vinegar, mayonnaise, mustard, salt, pepper, the remaining capers, the reserved potato cooking water and the reserved potato skins in a food processor or blender and process until well blended, about 1 minute. Pour over the potato mixture and mix well. Cover and refrigerate for at least 1 hour before serving. Serve chilled or at room temperature.

Wine Suggestion - Pinot Noir

Rice Salad

Sweet honey ham and salty olives are contrasted perfectly by the Honey Mustard Vinaigrette. Prepare it ahead of time and whisk it out for your lucky guests.

For the Rice Salad, cook the rice in 3 cups water, until just tender, 20 minutes for arborio rice or 15 minutes for other short grain rice. Transfer to a large bowl and cool completely.

Cook the carrot and celery in boiling water for 1 minute. Drain and rinse in cold water. Place in the bowl with the rice and add the remaining salad ingredients.

For the Honey Mustard Vinaigrette, whisk together all the ingredients in a medium bowl. Pour the vinaigrette over the rice and vegetables, tossing well. Cover and refrigerate for 1 hour. Serve chilled or at room temperature.

Wine Suggestion - Chenin Blanc

RICE SALAD

1½ cups short-grain rice, preferably arborio

1 carrot, peeled and cut into ¼-inch (6-mm) dice

1 stalk celery, cut into ¼-inch (6-mm) dice

½ cup frozen peas, thawed

½ red pepper, cut into ¼-inch (6-mm) dice

½ cup honey ham, cut into ¼-inch (6-mm) dice

1 (5¾-ounce) (163-g) can pitted large California black olives, quartered

HONEY MUSTARD VINAIGRETTE

¼ cup olive oil

¼ cup red wine vinegar

2 tablespoons honey mustard

¾ teaspoon salt

¼ teaspoon black pepper

1 garlic clove, finely chopped

2 tablespoons chopped fresh Italian parsley

2 tablespoons chopped fresh sage

PASTA and RICE

La Signora Izabela

At almost any time in my kitchen, a boiling pot of water for pasta will be raising a giant cloud of steam. And, as if by magic, I'll see a succession of smiling faces through this curtain of smoke - family and friends coming together at the dinner table to share a simple meal or a culinary adventure, and always a lively story or two.

My first memory of this love affair with pasta is my mother's spaghetti and meatballs. In fact, I cannot now remember a single day in the Stellino house when we did not have pasta with our meals, in one form or another. Pasta with Tomato Sauce, Ricotta and Romano Cheese transports me to weekends spent at grandma Maria's house; and Lasagne with Bolognese Sauce still satisfies my boyhood cravings.

I must admit that, in general, Italians are not very open to the culinary influences of foreign cultures, especially when it comes to pasta. Historical fact to the contrary, we believe that we invented it - or at least take the credit for raising the preparation of pasta to a high art form. For me, perhaps, it's the influence of many years living in the United States that has made me more receptive to new ways to cook and serve Italy's "national" food. I have found inspiration in many non-Italian cuisines and, most especially, from those of the neighboring countries of the Mediterranean.

I was introduced to my first foreign version of a pasta dish when I was a teenager holidaying with my parents in a small fishing village on the western tip of Sicily. We loved San Vito Lo Capo for its many sandy beaches and crystal blue-green sea that truly symbolizes the beauty of Sicily. We returned year after year to this sanctuary, along with other families from the big cities, many of whom we came to know well.

One summer, strangers rented the house next to the abandoned tuna factory on the cove. My brother, Mario, and I knew the house well from the many days spent swimming and fishing at the nearby beach. Most afternoons we'd make our way down to the cove by way of a small trail that wound past the strangers' house. Even after several weeks, all we knew of them was the sound of tunes sung in the sweet yet quavering voice of what had to be an older woman and the heady cooking smells that wafted from the open windows.

Early one day, I decided to go fishing alone at the cove. As I passed the house on my way down the trail, I saw an elderly gray-haired lady - the songbird, I guessed - on the terrace. She waved and nodded politely. Momentarily distracted, I tripped over a rock in the middle of the path and went crashing to the ground. Stunned, bruised and somewhat embarrassed, I looked up to see the old lady running down the path, displaying the athleticism of a woman half her age. She helped me to my feet and, in thickly accented Italian, insisted that I follow her to the house for first aid.

As she sat me down on the terrace, it was impossible to ignore the breathtaking view of the scenery below. The water was so clear and calm, I could see the fish swimming. The lady disappeared into the house, but returned in an instant with a cool glass of water and a steaming plate of pasta. Even in my discomfort, I inhaled the seductive aroma of the curry-spiced gnocchi. It was brimming with colorful red and yellow peppers, dotted with bright green peas and pieces of shrimp and scallops that shone under the afternoon sun. This was certainly *my* idea of first aid. With each bite, the aches and pains lessened.

My savior, it turned out, was La Signora Izabela, a Spaniard. We passed the afternoon sharing stories of our families. She and her Sicilian-born husband, Carmine, had for many years worked on the cruise ships that plied the Mediterranean. He worked as a waiter and she as a chef. Life had been an adventure for them. Their passion for each other and their love of travelling made for a blissful marriage. She told me how often Carmine had talked of his native Sicily with the woefulness of a long-lost love. His wish was to have the two things that he loved most in life together. So, after many years, here she was, singing and cooking in a little rented house on the shores of the sea that had once carried them so far away.

La Signora Izabela's wonderful Fisherman's Gnocchi, which I have tried to re-create in this book, opened my eyes to the unlimited culinary opportunities that lay just over the horizon. The following chapter is laden with a selection of my favorite pasta recipes. Many of these are based on traditional recipes infused with a range of Mediterranean flavors; and throughout, I have tried to simplify these dishes with uncomplicated cooking methods and readily available ingredients. I hope these recipes will bring wonderful pasta to your table with ease and speed ... but never at the expense of good taste.

Pasta Alfredo

This dish is an Italian specialty that has fans all over the world. Simple, yet quite elegant, it is an excellent choice for special occasions. You really do have to get the imported Parmigiano Reggiano cheese for the best results. Indulge yourself for once!

3 quarts (2.75 l) water

2½ cups whipping cream

8 garlic cloves, finely chopped

1 teaspoon salt

¼ teaspoon black pepper

1 cup freshly grated
  Parmigiano Reggiano
  cheese

1 pound (450 g) pasta -
  fettuccine, tagliatelle,
  ravioli, tortellini
  or tortiglioni

3 tablespoons chopped fresh
  Italian parsley

¼ cup shaved Parmigiano
  Reggiano cheese

Bring the water to a boil in a large pot. Heat the cream, garlic, salt and pepper in a medium saucepan set on medium heat until it reaches a simmer, about 7 minutes. Continue to simmer the cream mixture until it has reduced to 2 cups, about 15 minutes. Stir the mixture occasionally to keep the garlic from sticking to the bottom of the pan. When the sauce has reduced, remove it from the heat and stir in the 1 cup of grated cheese.

While the sauce is reducing, cook the pasta in the boiling water until just tender. Drain the pasta and transfer it to a large serving bowl. Pour the sauce over the pasta and toss well. Sprinkle with the chopped parsley and the shaved cheese and serve.

Cook's Tip

For an absolutely sinful addition to this traditional dish, stir 2 tablespoons of truffle oil into the sauce before tossing it with the pasta.

Wine Suggestion - Sauvignon Blanc

Pasta with Sun-dried Tomatoes and Pine Nuts

If you keep sun-dried tomatoes and pine nuts in your cupboard, you can throw this dinner together at a moment's notice. Quick and simple, the tomatoes and nuts give this vegetarian dish a substantial meaty feeling. It reminds me of being in the countryside of Sicily.

Bring the water to a boil in a large pot. Add the olive oil, garlic, red pepper flakes, pine nuts, sun-dried tomatoes and onion to a large sauté pan set on high heat. Cook until the onion is soft and the garlic is beginning to brown, about 3 minutes. Stir in the wine and boil until the wine is reduced by half, about 1-2 minutes. Pour in the chicken stock, salt and pepper and bring to a boil. Reduce the heat to medium and simmer for 7 minutes, until the sauce is slightly thickened.

While the sauce is simmering, cook the pasta in the boiling water until just tender. Drain the pasta well and return it to the pot. Pour the sauce over the pasta and cook over medium heat for 3 minutes, stirring constantly. Remove from the heat, stir in the cheese and serve.

Wine Suggestion - Sauvignon Blanc

3 quarts (2.75 l) water

3 tablespoons olive oil

6 garlic cloves, thickly sliced

¼ teaspoon red pepper flakes

½ cup pine nuts

1 cup sliced oil-packed
    sun-dried tomatoes

½ onion, chopped

½ cup dry white wine

1½ cups Chicken Stock
    (see page 225)

¾ teaspoon salt

¼ teaspoon black pepper

1 pound (450 g) pasta -
    spaghetti, penne, ravioli
    or tortellini

¼ cup freshly grated
    Pecorino Romano cheese

Pasta with Zucchini, Eggplant and Tomatoes

⌄

SERVES 4 TO 6

I am not a vegetarian by any means, but I assure you that the smoky, rich eggplant in this dish, tossed with tomatoes, zucchini and fresh herbs, provides complete satisfaction.

½ pound (225 g) eggplant, cut into ½-inch (1.5-cm) dice

1 teaspoon salt

3 quarts (2.75 l) water

5 tablespoons olive oil

1 pound (450 g) zucchini, cut into ½-inch (1.5-cm) dice

4 garlic cloves, thickly sliced

¼ teaspoon red pepper flakes

1 tablespoon chopped fresh Italian parsley

1 tablespoon chopped fresh basil or 1 teaspoon dried

2 tablespoons chopped fresh mint

1 (28-ounce) (790-g) can peeled Italian tomatoes, drained, chopped and juices reserved separately

¼ teaspoon black pepper

1 pound (450 g) pasta - tortellini, tortelloni or penne rigate

4 tablespoons freshly grated Pecorino Romano cheese

Sprinkle the eggplant with ¼ teaspoon of the salt and place in a colander. Put a plate on top of the eggplant and weight it down with several cans to help squeeze the bitter juices from the eggplant. Drain for 15 minutes and pat dry.

Bring the water to a boil in a large pot. In a large sauté pan set on high heat, heat the olive oil until sizzling, about 2 minutes. Cook the eggplant and zucchini until they begin to brown, about 3 minutes. Add the garlic, red pepper flakes, parsley, basil and mint and cook for 2 minutes, stirring occasionally. Stir in the chopped tomatoes and cook for 2 minutes. Add the reserved tomato juices, the remaining salt and the pepper and simmer for 4-5 minutes.

Cook the pasta in the boiling water until just tender. Drain well and return to the pot. Pour the sauce over the pasta and cook over medium heat for 3 minutes, stirring constantly. Remove the pan from the heat and stir in the cheese before serving.

Wine Suggestion - Merlot

Pasta with Vegetable Ragú

This pasta is ablaze with color. It may take a little extra effort to dice the vegetables very small, but it is this small cut that gives the sauce its unique texture and appearance.

Bring the water to a boil in a large pot. Heat 2 tablespoons of the olive oil in a large sauté pan set on high heat until sizzling, about 2 minutes. Cook the asparagus, zucchini and squash for 3-4 minutes, until well browned. Transfer to a bowl and set aside.

Reduce the heat to medium-high and add the remaining olive oil to the same pan. Cook the garlic, shallots or onion, red pepper flakes and thyme for 1 minute, until the garlic and shallots or onion begin to brown. Return the cooked vegetables to the pan and stir well. Pour the wine into the pan and boil until reduced by half, about 2 minutes. Add the peas, chicken stock, tomato sauce, salt and pepper and bring to a boil. Reduce the heat to medium and simmer for 4-5 minutes.

While the sauce is simmering, cook the pasta in the boiling water until just tender. Drain the pasta well and return it to the pot. Pour the sauce over the pasta and cook over medium heat for 3 minutes, stirring constantly. Stir in the cheese and the butter, if you wish. Sprinkle each serving with the chopped basil.

Cook's Tip

For a more elegant presentation, toss the pasta with just three-quarters of the sauce. Top each serving with the remaining sauce and sprinkle with the basil and cheese.

Wine Suggestion - Chardonnay

3 quarts (2.75 l) water

4 tablespoons olive oil

1 pound (450 g) asparagus, cut into ½-inch (1.5-cm) pieces

1 zucchini, cut into ½-inch (1.5-cm) dice

1 yellow squash, cut into ½-inch (1.5-cm) dice

4 garlic cloves, finely chopped

¼ cup finely chopped shallots or white onion

¼ teaspoon red pepper flakes

2 teaspoons thyme

¼ cup dry white wine

½ cup frozen peas, thawed

1 cup Chicken Stock (see page 225)

¾ cup Tomato Sauce (see page 222)

¾ teaspoon salt

¼ teaspoon black pepper

1 pound (450 g) pasta - spaghetti or spaghettini

¼ cup freshly grated Parmigiano Reggiano cheese

1 tablespoon butter (optional)

4 tablespoons chopped fresh basil

Pasta with Tomato Sauce, Ricotta and Romano Cheese

↓

SERVES 4 TO 6

Perfect when you want something quick to assemble and yet very tasty. You'll notice how the ricotta cheese is a great way to contrast the Romano cheese's salty quality.

3 quarts (2.75 l) water

3 tablespoons olive oil

¼ teaspoon red pepper flakes

4 garlic cloves, thickly sliced

1 (28-ounce) (790-g) can
   peeled Italian tomatoes,
   drained, chopped and
   juices reserved separately

4 tablespoons chopped fresh
   basil or 4 teaspoons dried

¾ teaspoon salt

1 pound (450 g) pasta -
   penne rigate, tortiglioni,
   ziti or rigatoni

½ cup ricotta cheese

½ cup freshly grated
   Pecorino Romano cheese

½ teaspoon black pepper
   (or to taste)

3 tablespoons chopped fresh
   Italian parsley

Bring the water to a boil in a large pot. Heat the olive oil, red pepper flakes and garlic in a large sauté pan set on medium-high heat, until it begins to sizzle and the garlic begins to brown, about 2 minutes. Add the drained tomatoes, basil and salt and cook for 2 minutes. Stir in the reserved tomato juices and bring to a boil. Reduce the heat to medium and simmer for 5 minutes.

While the sauce is simmering, cook the pasta in the boiling water until just tender. Drain the pasta well and return it to the pot. Pour the sauce over the pasta and cook over medium heat for 3 minutes, stirring constantly. Remove the pot from the heat and stir in the ricotta cheese and Romano cheese, mixing well.

Serve the pasta sprinkled with the black pepper and chopped parsley.

Cook's Tip

For an interesting variation that adds a nice zip, add 4 tablespoons of chopped oil-packed sun-dried tomatoes to the pan when you add the chopped tomatoes.

Wine Suggestion - Merlot

Pasta with Spicy Cauliflower Sauce

This dish is the best way to slip cauliflower into dinner. It is expertly hidden with just the right amounts of anchovy, garlic, red pepper flakes and sweet basil. A sprinkle of bread crumbs and cheese at the end gives it a final flourish of aroma and texture.

Grease a 9 x 13-inch (23 x 33-cm) baking dish and set aside. Bring the water to a boil in a large pot. Heat the olive oil, garlic, anchovy paste, red pepper flakes and black pepper in a large sauté pan set on high heat, until the olive oil begins to sizzle and the garlic begins to brown, about 2 minutes. Add the cauliflower and 1 tablespoon of the chopped basil (or 1 teaspoon dried) and cook until the cauliflower begins to brown, about 4 minutes.

Add the pasta to the boiling water and cook until just tender. Scoop 1 cup of water from the pot of cooking pasta and add it to the pan of cauliflower along with the salt. Reduce the heat to medium and cook for 4-5 minutes, until the sauce is slightly thickened. Preheat the broiler.

Drain the pasta well and return it to the pot. Stir in the sauce, half the cheese and the remaining basil. Pour the pasta into the greased baking dish and sprinkle with the bread crumbs and the remaining cheese. Place under the broiler for 5-6 minutes, until the bread crumbs and cheese are golden brown. Sprinkle with the chopped parsley and serve family style.

Wine Suggestion - Gewürztraminer

3 quarts (2.75 l) water

5 tablespoons olive oil

6 garlic cloves, thickly sliced

1 tablespoon anchovy paste

½ teaspoon red pepper flakes

¼ teaspoon black pepper

1 pound (450 g) cauliflower florets, cut into 1-inch (2.5-cm) pieces

3 tablespoons chopped fresh basil or 1 tablespoon dried

1 pound (450 g) pasta - penne rigate, tortiglioni or rigatoni

1 cup pasta cooking water (see directions)

½ teaspoon salt

½ cup freshly grated Pecorino Romano cheese

¼ cup Italian Bread Crumbs (see page 230)

2 tablespoons chopped fresh Italian parsley

Pasta with Artichoke and Leek Sauce

SERVES 4 TO 6

Smooth and silky, this creamy pasta is the right choice for a gentle evening. Since the recipe calls for only half a package of artichokes, dice the remaining hearts and sprinkle them over the top just before serving.

3 quarts (2.75 l) water

3 tablespoons olive oil

4 garlic cloves, thickly sliced

¼ teaspoon red pepper flakes

3 artichoke hearts, thinly sliced
   or half of 1 (9-ounce)
   (250-g) package frozen
   artichoke hearts,
   thinly sliced

1 cup sliced leeks, white
   part only

3 tablespoons chopped fresh
   Italian parsley

¼ cup dry white wine

1½ cups Vegetable or Chicken
   Stock (see page 223 or 225)

⅓ cup whipping cream

¾ teaspoon salt

¼ teaspoon black pepper

1 pound (450 g) pasta - penne
   rigate, rigatoni, tortiglioni,
   tortellini or gnocchi

1 tablespoon butter

¼ cup freshly grated
   Parmigiano Reggiano cheese

Bring the water to a boil in a large pot. Heat the olive oil in a large sauté pan set on high heat until sizzling, about 2 minutes. Add the garlic, red pepper flakes, artichokes, leeks, and parsley and cook until the garlic begins to brown, about 2-3 minutes. Pour in the wine and boil until reduced by half, about 1-2 minutes. Add the vegetable or chicken stock, cream, salt and pepper and bring to a boil. Reduce the heat to medium and cook, covered, until the artichokes are so soft they break with pressure from the back of a spoon, about 5-7 minutes. Purée the artichoke mixture in a food processor or blender to a creamy consistency. Set aside.

Cook the pasta in the boiling water until just tender. Drain the pasta well and return it to the pot. Pour the puréed sauce over the pasta and cook over medium heat for 3 minutes, stirring constantly. Remove from the heat and stir in the butter and cheese. The pasta is ready to be served.

Wine Suggestion - Chardonnay

Pasta with Golden Pepper Sauce

Everyone will comment on the golden color of this sauce - very bright, warm and dramatic. Serve it for a special occasion and make sure to use the sparkling wine or champagne for the height of taste.

Bring the water to a boil in a large pot. Heat the olive oil in a large sauté pan set on high heat until sizzling, about 2 minutes. Add the garlic, red pepper flakes, thyme, salt, pepper, bell peppers and ham and cook for 4-5 minutes.

Pour the champagne or wine into the pan of peppers and boil until reduced by half, about 1-2 minutes. Reduce the heat to medium and add the roasted red pepper, saffron or turmeric, cream, bouillon cube and chicken stock. Bring to a boil and simmer for 5-7 minutes, until the sauce is slightly thickened.

While the sauce is simmering, cook the pasta in the boiling water until just tender. Drain the pasta well and return to the pot. Pour the sauce over the pasta and cook over medium heat for 3 minutes, stirring constantly. Remove from the heat and stir in the butter and cheese. Sprinkle each serving with the chopped parsley.

Wine Suggestion - Gewürztraminer

3 quarts (2.75 l) water
4 tablespoons olive oil
4 garlic cloves, thickly sliced
¼ teaspoon red pepper flakes
1 teaspoon thyme
¾ teaspoon salt
¼ teaspoon black pepper
2 yellow bell peppers, cut into fine dice (makes 2½ cups diced pepper)
1 cup finely diced smoked ham
½ cup champagne, sparkling wine or white still wine
½ cup finely diced roasted red pepper (from a jar)
¼ teaspoon saffron powder or turmeric
⅓ cup whipping cream
½ chicken bouillon cube
¾ cup Chicken Stock (see page 225)
1 pound (450 g) pasta - penne rigate, rigatoni, tortiglioni or farfalle
1 tablespoon butter
4 tablespoons freshly grated Parmigiano Reggiano cheese
3 tablespoons chopped fresh Italian parsley

Pasta with Vegetables and Pesto Sauce

Pesto sauces are one of the most universally accepted exports from the Mediterranean. This pesto's bright green color explodes with fresh basil flavor. The potatoes and green beans are a hearty addition that provide wonderful bite. It's simply flavorful and easy to make.

PESTO SAUCE
MAKES 1 CUP

1 cup fresh, firmly packed, basil leaves, washed and dried

2 peeled garlic cloves

½ cup pine nuts

½ cup freshly grated Parmigiano Reggiano cheese

¾ teaspoon salt

¼ teaspoon black pepper

⅓ cup extra virgin olive oil

PASTA AND VEGETABLES

3 quarts (2.75 l) water

2 teaspoons salt

1 pound (450 g) pasta - egg tagliatelle, gnocchi, penne rigate, linguine or lingue di passero

½ pound (225 g) red new potatoes, unpeeled, finely diced

¼ pound (115 g) green beans, cut into medium dice

For the Pesto Sauce, process the basil, garlic and pine nuts to a smooth paste in a food processor. Add the cheese, salt and pepper and pulse to mix well. With the machine running, add the olive oil in a slow stream until completely mixed. Set aside.

For the Pasta and Vegetables, bring the water to a boil in a large pot. Add the salt and pasta and cook until the pasta is just tender. Add the potatoes to the pasta during the last 5 minutes of cooking and the green beans during the last 3 minutes. Drain the pasta and vegetables well and put in a large pasta bowl. Pour in the sauce and stir well. Serve immediately.

Cook's Tip

If you can't find pine nuts or the cost is prohibitive, almonds are a great substitution. Use ½ cup sliced almonds and increase the olive oil to ½ cup.

Wine Suggestion - Cabernet Sauvignon

Spinach Lasagne

Once you master the simple art of layering lasagne noodles with filling ingredients, there's no end to the combinations you'll discover. This vegetarian version combines hearty chopped spinach with creamy béchamel sauce and zippy tomato sauce. Any leftovers will just taste better the next day.

Bring the water to a boil in a large pot. Cook the lasagne noodles according to package directions. Drain and lay them flat on a baking sheet. Use 2 tablespoons of the olive oil to brush both sides of the noodles. Set aside.

In a large bowl, stir the spinach, ricotta cheese, garlic, eggs, nutmeg, salt and pepper until creamy. The ingredients can also be processed in a food processor for 1-2 minutes.

Preheat the oven to 350°F (180°C). To assemble the lasagne, grease a 9 x 13-inch (23 x 33-cm) baking dish with the remaining olive oil. Place one-quarter of the noodles across the bottom of the dish, overlapping, if necessary, to fit.

Spread the following ingredients evenly over the top, trying to cover as much of the surface as possible: 1 cup of the tomato sauce, one-third of the spinach mixture, ½ cup of the béchamel sauce and ½ cup of the Parmigiano Reggiano cheese. Repeat the noodle and filling layers 2 more times.

The top layer is simply the remaining noodles (use all the noodles), the remaining 1½ cups of the béchamel sauce and the remaining ½ cup of the Parmigiano Reggiano cheese.

Cover the lasagne loosely with aluminum foil and bake for 1 hour. Remove the foil and bake an additional 30 minutes, until the sides are bubbling and the top is golden brown. Remove from the oven and let sit for 10 minutes before serving. Cut into large squares and enjoy!

Wine Suggestion - Semillon-Chardonnay

1 pound (450 g) lasagne noodles

3 tablespoons olive oil

3 (10-ounce) (300-g) packages frozen chopped spinach, thawed and squeezed of excess moisture

1½ cups ricotta cheese

8 garlic cloves, finely chopped

2 eggs

¼ teaspoon nutmeg

1½ teaspoons salt

¾ teaspoon black pepper

3 cups Tomato Sauce (see page 222)

3 cups Béchamel Sauce (see page 228)

2 cups freshly grated Parmigiano Reggiano cheese

Timbale of Pasta Margherita

Mozzarella and Romano cheeses, combined with stewed tomatoes and basil, give this dish great flavor. It takes a little extra time, but it's worth the effort for the dramatic final appearance.

2 (1½-pound) (700-g)
    eggplants

2 teaspoons salt

7 tablespoons olive oil

3 quarts (2.75 l) water

1 pound (450 g) pasta -
    penne or rigatoni

6 garlic cloves, thickly sliced

2 cups sliced leeks, white part
    only (4 leeks)

¼ teaspoon red pepper flakes

2 (14½-ounce) (415-g) cans
    Italian stewed tomatoes,
    drained, chopped and
    juices reserved separately

¼ teaspoon black pepper

4 tablespoons chopped
    fresh basil

⅓ cup Italian Bread Crumbs
    (see page 230)

16 ounces (450 g) grated
    mozzarella cheese (4 cups)

1 cup freshly grated
    Pecorino Romano cheese

Slice the eggplants lengthwise into thin slices. Sprinkle with 1½ teaspoons of the salt and lay the slices on top of one another in a large colander. Place a dish on top and weight it down (2 large cans of tomatoes work well). Drain for 20 minutes and pat dry with paper towels.

Preheat the oven to 425°F (220°C). Brush a nonstick baking sheet and the eggplant slices with 3 tablespoons of the olive oil and cook for 25 minutes, until lightly browned. Set aside.

Bring the water to a boil in a large pot. Heat 3 tablespoons of the remaining oil in a large sauté pan set on high heat until sizzling, about 2 minutes. Add the garlic, leeks and red pepper flakes and cook until the garlic begins to brown, about 2 minutes. Stir in the drained tomatoes and cook for 2 minutes. Add the tomato juices, the remaining salt and the pepper and bring to a boil. Reduce the heat to medium and cook for 4-5 minutes, until the sauce is slightly thickened.

Cook the pasta in the boiling water for three-quarters of the recommended cooking time (the pasta will finish cooking in the oven). Drain the pasta and return it to the pot. Toss the pasta with the sauce and the basil and set aside.

Preheat the oven to 400°F (200°C). Grease a 4-quart (3.75-l) ovenproof glass bowl with the remaining 1 tablespoon oil and then coat with the bread crumbs. Line the bowl with the roasted eggplant slices, overlapping them slightly. It's okay to have some overhang along the edge of the bowl.

Layer the bowl with one-third of the pasta mixture, 2 cups of the mozzarella cheese and ½ cup of the Romano cheese. Repeat the layer once more, then finish with the remaining pasta. Fold any overhanging eggplant over the top of the pasta, then top with more eggplant slices to cover. Cover the bowl with aluminum foil and bake for 30 minutes. Remove the foil and bake for another 30 minutes. Remove from the oven and let sit for 10 minutes. Invert the pasta onto a serving platter, cut into wedges and serve family style.

Wine Suggestion - Merlot

Leave it to a Sicilian chef to create a dish with such an eruption of flavor and texture - a true culinary Mt. Vesuvius.

Baked Pasta with Asparagus

So mellow and comforting, this great casserole-style pasta is perfect for the family, especially young children - an Italian version of America's classic macaroni and cheese.

3 quarts (2.75 l) water

4 tablespoons olive oil

4 garlic cloves, thickly sliced

¼ teaspoon red pepper flakes

½ white onion, thinly sliced

¾ cup frozen peas, thawed

1 pound (450 g) fresh
   asparagus, cut into large
   pieces

½ cup dry white wine

3 tablespoons chopped fresh
   Italian parsley

¾ teaspoon salt

¼ teaspoon black pepper

1½ cups Vegetable or Chicken
   Stock (see page 223 or
   225)

½ cup whipping cream

1 pound (450 g) pasta - penne

12 ounces (350 g) grated
   mozzarella cheese
   (approximately 3 cups)

¾ cup freshly grated
   Parmigiano Reggiano
   cheese

½ cup Italian Bread Crumbs
   (see page 230)

Bring the water to a boil in a large pot. In a large sauté pan set on high heat, heat the olive oil until sizzling, about 2 minutes. Add the garlic, red pepper flakes, onion, peas and asparagus and cook until the garlic begins to brown, about 2 minutes. Add the wine and boil until reduced by half, 1-2 minutes. Stir in the parsley, salt, pepper, vegetable or chicken stock and the cream and bring to a boil. Reduce the heat to simmer and cook for 5-7 minutes, until the sauce is slightly thickened.

While the sauce is simmering, cook the pasta in the boiling water for three-quarters of the recommended cooking time (the pasta will finish cooking in the oven). Drain the pasta well and return to the pot. Pour the finished sauce over the pasta and cook over medium heat, stirring constantly, for 3 minutes.

Preheat the oven to 350° F (180° C). Grease a 9 x 13-inch (23 x 33-cm) baking dish and spoon one-third of the pasta evenly over the bottom of the dish. Top with one-third of the mozzarella cheese, then one-third of the Parmigiano Reggiano cheese. Repeat these layers 2 more times. Sprinkle the bread crumbs over the top and bake for 30 minutes, until the top is golden brown. Remove the pasta from the oven and let sit for 10-15 minutes before serving.

Wine Suggestion - Cabernet Franc

Spaghetti and Meatballs

My meatball recipe has secret Stellino techniques that make them a standout. The combination of three different ground meats adds great depth of flavor. The milk gives the meatballs their tender texture while simmering the meatballs in the tomato sauce gives added zest. Enjoy!

For the Meatballs, mix all the ingredients except the ground meat and the olive oil in a large bowl. Add the ground beef, veal and pork and, with your hands, mix until all the ingredients are completely incorporated. Shape the mixture into oval meatballs, using 2 heaping tablespoons for each ball. This will make 32-34 meatballs.

Heat the olive oil in a large sauté pan set on high heat until sizzling, about 2 minutes. Brown the meatballs for 2-3 minutes on each side. Don't crowd the meatballs in the pan when browning, you will need to brown them in several batches. Remove the meatballs from the pan and drain on paper towels or brown paper bags. Repeat with the remaining meatballs. Set aside.

For the Spaghetti and Sauce, bring the water to a boil in a large pot. Drain the olive oil from the pan above and add the tomato sauce, beef stock, salt and pepper, stirring well. Return the meatballs to the pan and bring the liquid to a boil. Reduce the heat to medium and cook for 15 minutes.

While the sauce is simmering, add the pasta to the boiling water and cook until just tender. Drain the pasta well and return it to the pot. Add half the sauce from the meatball pan and toss it with the pasta. Transfer the pasta to a large serving bowl or platter and top with the meatballs and the remaining sauce. Sprinkle with the chopped parsley and serve.

Wine Suggestion - Syrah

MEATBALLS
½ cup milk
2 tablespoons finely chopped garlic
¼ cup chopped fresh Italian parsley
½ cup Italian Bread Crumbs (see page 230)
2 eggs
2 cups freshly grated Pecorino Romano cheese
2 tablespoons sugar
1 teaspoon cinnamon
1 teaspoon nutmeg
½ teaspoon black pepper
⅔ pound (300 g) lean ground beef
⅔ pound (300 g) ground veal
⅔ pound (300 g) ground pork
2 tablespoons olive oil

SPAGHETTI AND SAUCE
3 quarts (2.75 l) water
3 cups Tomato Sauce (see page 222)
½ cup Beef Stock (see page 226)
1 teaspoon salt
½ teaspoon black pepper
1 pound (450 g) pasta - spaghetti, rigatoni, ziti or tortiglioni
2 tablespoons chopped fresh Italian parsley

Cannelloni with Prosciutto and Zucchini

Everyone loves cannelloni, probably because you can fill it with whatever strikes your fancy. This combination of zucchini, garlic, cheese and ham is full of flavor, but not overly rich. It may seem like too much zucchini, but they cook down quite a bit. (Illustrated on the opposite page.)

3 quarts (2.75 l) water

12 cannelloni shells

3 tablespoons olive oil

4 medium zucchini, diced

8 garlic cloves, thickly sliced

¼ teaspoon red pepper flakes

½ onion, chopped

½ teaspoon salt

¼ teaspoon black pepper

¼ cup white wine

¼ cup Chicken Stock
(see page 225)

1 cup ricotta cheese

⅔ cup freshly grated
Parmigiano Reggiano
cheese

¾ cup chopped prosciutto
or ham

¼ cup chopped fresh
Italian parsley

2 cups Tomato Sauce
(see page 222)

¾ cup Béchamel Sauce
(see page 228)

Bring the water to a boil in a large pot. Cook the cannelloni shells for half the time directed on the package. Drain the shells and place them on a baking sheet to cool.

Preheat the oven to 400° F (200° C). Heat the olive oil in a large sauté pan set on high heat until sizzling, about 2 minutes. Add the zucchini, garlic, red pepper flakes, onion, salt and pepper and cook about 8-10 minutes. Add the wine and chicken stock and boil until most of the liquid cooks away, about 4-5 minutes. Place the zucchini mixture in a food processor with the ricotta, ⅓ cup of the Parmigiano Reggiano cheese, the prosciutto and parsley and process to a smooth consistency.

Transfer the filling to a piping bag with a large open tip. Place the tip in one end of the cannelloni and fill halfway. Place the tip in the other end of the shell and finish filling. Repeat with the remaining shells. If you don't have a piping bag, cut each cannelloni shell open lengthwise, lay on a flat surface and spoon 2-3 tablespoons of the filling down the center. Roll the shell up and set aside until you've filled the remaining shells.

Pour 1 cup of the tomato sauce over the bottom of a 9 x 13-inch (23 x 33-cm) baking dish or casserole. Place the filled cannelloni on top of the sauce. (If you've split the cannelloni shells, place them in the dish seam-side-down.) Pour the remaining tomato sauce over the cannelloni, top with the béchamel sauce and sprinkle with the remaining Parmigiano Reggiano cheese. Bake for 30-40 minutes. Remove from the oven and let sit for 10 minutes before serving.

Wine Suggestion - Pinot Noir

OPPOSITE: (TOP) LASAGNE WITH BOLOGNESE MEAT SAUCE (PAGE 90), (BOTTOM) CANNELLONI WITH PROSCIUTTO AND ZUCCHINI (PAGE 88).

Pasta with Lima Beans and Swiss Chard

⌄

SERVES 4 TO 6

I found that the name of this dish made people suspicious that they were being prepared some "eat-it-because-vegetables-are-good-for-you" meal. I just love watching people taste it, and then keep coming back for seconds until the serving dish is empty! (Illustrated on the opposite page.)

Bring the water to a boil in a large pot. Heat the olive oil in a large sauté pan set on high heat until sizzling, about 2 minutes. Add the garlic, red pepper flakes, parsley, onion, lima beans and prosciutto or ham. Reduce the heat to medium and cook until the garlic begins to brown and the onion is soft, about 5-6 minutes. Stir in the wine and boil until reduced by half, about 2 minutes. Add the chicken stock, cream, salt and pepper and simmer for 10-15 minutes, until the sauce is slightly thickened. Add the Swiss chard or spinach leaves to the sauce about 2 minutes before it's done, stirring well.

While the sauce is simmering, add the pasta to the boiling water and cook until just tender. Drain the pasta well and return it to the pot. Pour the sauce over the pasta and cook over medium heat, stirring constantly, for 3 minutes. Remove the pan from the heat, stir in the cheese and serve.

Wine Suggestion - Cabernet Sauvignon

3 quarts (2.75 l) water

3 tablespoons olive oil

6 garlic cloves, thickly sliced

¼ teaspoon red pepper flakes

2 tablespoons chopped fresh Italian parsley

½ onion, chopped

1½ cups frozen lima beans, thawed

¾ cup chopped prosciutto or ham

¼ cup dry white wine

1½ cups Chicken Stock (see page 225)

⅓ cup whipping cream

¾ teaspoon salt

¼ teaspoon black pepper

3 cups thinly sliced Swiss chard or spinach leaves

1 pound (450 g) pasta - penne, ravioli, tortiglioni or spaghetti

¼ cup freshly grated Parmigiano Reggiano cheese

OPPOSITE: PASTA WITH LIMA BEANS AND SWISS CHARD (PAGE 89).
PREVIOUS PAGES: PAELLA VALENCIANA (PAGES 96-97).

Lasagne with Bolognese Meat Sauce

This is one of my most requested recipes. One mouthful of its great meaty flavor, combined with the rich sauce, and you'll understand why it's a favorite around the world. (Illustrated in this section.)

3 quarts (2.75 l) water

1 pound (450 g) lasagne noodles

3 tablespoons olive oil

4½ cups Bolognese Meat Sauce (see page 227)

3 cups Béchamel Sauce (see page 228)

2 cups freshly grated Parmigiano Reggiano cheese

Bring the water to a boil in a large pot and cook the lasagne noodles according to package directions. Drain the noodles and lay them flat on a baking sheet. Use 2 tablespoons of the olive oil to brush both sides of the noodles. Set aside to cool.

Preheat the oven to 350° F (180° C). To assemble the lasagne, grease a 9 x 13-inch (23 x 33-cm) baking dish with the remaining olive oil. Place one-quarter of the noodles across the bottom of the dish, overlapping if necessary, to fit.

Spread the following filling ingredients evenly over the top, trying to cover as much of the surface as possible: 1½ cups of the Bolognese meat sauce, ½ cup of the béchamel sauce and ½ cup of the Parmigiano Reggiano cheese. Repeat the noodle and filling layer 2 more times.

The top layer is simply the remaining noodles (use all the noodles) covered with the remaining 1½ cups of béchamel sauce and sprinkled with the remaining ½ cup of Parmigiano Reggiano cheese.

Cover the lasagne loosely with aluminum foil and bake for 1 hour. Remove the foil and bake an additional 30 minutes, until the sides are bubbling and the top is golden brown. Remove from the oven and let sit for 10 minutes before serving. To serve, cut into large squares and serve.

Wine Suggestion - Merlot

Pasta with Salami and Ricotta

Such a simple yet satisfying dinner! There is great spice and heartiness from the salami, but the ricotta cheese really smooths it out and enriches the sauce. Substitute pepperoni for the salami, if you wish. I think children will love this because the salami or pepperoni will remind them of pizza!

Bring the water to a boil in a large pot. Heat the olive oil in a large sauté pan set on high heat until sizzling, about 2 minutes. Add the garlic, red pepper flakes, onion, salami and oregano and cook until the garlic begins to brown, about 3 minutes. Pour in the wine and boil until the wine is reduced by half, about 1-2 minutes. Add the tomato sauce, chicken stock, salt and pepper and bring to a boil. Reduce the heat to medium and simmer for 10-12 minutes, until the sauce is slightly thickened.

While the sauce is simmering, cook the pasta in the boiling water until just tender. Drain well and return to the pot. Pour the sauce over the pasta and cook over medium heat for 3 minutes, stirring constantly. Remove the pot from the heat, stir in the Romano and ricotta cheeses and the pasta is ready to serve.

Wine Suggestion - Cabernet Franc

3 quarts (2.75 l) water

3 tablespoons olive oil

4 garlic cloves, thickly sliced

¼ teaspoon red pepper flakes

½ onion, chopped

1 cup (4 ounces) (115 g) chopped Italian salami, firmly packed (soppressata, Napoli, Genova)

½ teaspoon oregano

¼ cup dry red wine

¾ cup Tomato Sauce (see page 222)

¾ cup Chicken Stock (see page 225)

¼ teaspoon salt

¼ teaspoon black pepper

1 pound (450 g) pasta - penne rigate, tortiglioni, ziti or tortellini

¼ cup freshly grated Pecorino Romano cheese

½ cup ricotta cheese

Gnocchi with Creamy Asparagus-Prosciutto Sauce

Gnocchi, asparagus and prosciutto are three of my most favorite ingredients. Gnocchi is a noodle with a distinctive potato base. Look for this Italian speciality in the pasta section of your supermarket.

3 quarts (2.75 l) water

3 tablespoons olive oil

4 garlic cloves, thickly sliced

½ cup chopped white onion

1 pound (450 g) asparagus, tops cut off and reserved separately, stems cut into ½-inch (1.5-cm) pieces

¼ cup dry white wine

2 tablespoons chopped fresh Italian parsley

1¼ cups Chicken Stock (see page 225)

¾ teaspoon salt

¼ teaspoon black pepper

½ cup prosciutto or thinly sliced smoked ham, cut into thin strips

⅓ cup whipping cream

2 (1-pound) (450-g) packages gnocchi or 1 pound (450 g) pasta - penne rigate, rigatoni, tortiglioni or ziti

¼ cup freshly grated Parmigiano Reggiano cheese

Bring the water to a boil in a large pot. Heat 2 tablespoons of the olive oil in a large sauté pan set on high heat until sizzling, about 2 minutes. Add the garlic, onion and asparagus stems and cook until the garlic begins to brown, about 2 minutes. Pour in the wine and boil until reduced by half, about 2 minutes. Add the parsley, chicken stock, salt and pepper and bring to a boil. Reduce the heat to medium and simmer, covered, for 5 minutes, until the asparagus is soft.

Transfer the asparagus mixture to a food processor or blender and process to a smooth, creamy consistency, about 1 minute.

In the same pan, heat the remaining olive oil over medium-high heat until sizzling, about 1 minute. Add the asparagus tops and half the prosciutto or ham and cook for 2-3 minutes, until the prosciutto or ham and asparagus begin to change color and become fragrant. Add the processed asparagus mixture and the cream to the pan, reduce the heat to medium and simmer for 5 minutes.

While the sauce is simmering, cook the gnocchi or pasta in the boiling water according to package directions, drain well and return to the pot. Pour the sauce over the gnocchi, add the cheese and gently stir to coat well. Transfer to plates and top each serving with the remaining prosciutto or ham.

Wine Suggestion - Syrah

Fisherman's Gnocchi

I love the way the fresh seafood flavors pair up with the golden curry powder in this recipe to make a rich and elegant pasta dinner. The splash of brandy helps to bring out a spectacular new side of the seafood.

Bring the water to a boil in a large pot. Heat 2 tablespoons of the olive oil in a large sauté pan set on high heat until sizzling, about 2 minutes. Add the shrimp and scallops and cook until the shrimp starts to turn pink and the scallops lightly brown on the edges, about 1-2 minutes. Remove to a dish and set aside.

Add the remaining olive oil to the same pan and cook the garlic, red pepper flakes, onion and bell pepper on high heat, until the garlic begins to brown, about 2-3 minutes. Stir in the curry powder, salt and pepper and cook for 1 minute. Pour in the brandy and boil until reduced by half, about 1-2 minutes. Stir in the tomato sauce, shrimp stock or clam juice, cream, peas and basil and bring to a boil. Reduce the heat to simmer and cook for 5 minutes.

While the sauce is simmering, cook the gnocchi or pasta in the boiling water according to package directions. Drain well and return to the pot. Return the shrimp and scallops to the sauce to reheat. Pour the sauce over the gnocchi and stir gently until well coated. If using pasta, cook over medium heat for 3 minutes, stirring constantly. Serve immediately.

Wine Suggestion - Chardonnay

3 quarts (2.75 l) water
4 tablespoons olive oil
¾ pound (350 g) medium shrimp (16-20 count), shelled and deveined
¾ pound (350 g) sea scallops, cut in half horizontally
4 garlic cloves, thickly sliced
¼ teaspoon red pepper flakes
½ onion, chopped
1 red or yellow bell pepper (or half of each), cut into medium dice
¾ teaspoon curry powder
¾ teaspoon salt
¼ teaspoon black pepper
¼ cup brandy
½ cup Tomato Sauce (see page 222)
¾ cup Shrimp Stock (see page 224) or clam juice
⅓ cup whipping cream
½ cup frozen peas, thawed
3 tablespoons chopped fresh basil or 1 tablespoon dried
1 pound (450 g) pasta - gnocchi or penne, rigatoni, ziti or tortiglioni

Pasta with Shrimp and Zucchini

SERVES 4 TO 6

Succulent pink shrimp, tossed with light green zucchini and a rich golden yellow saffron sauce, is a perfect summer celebration. Rock shrimp are preferable in this recipe because of their tender texture. However, they are also a bit saltier, so you may want to wait until the end of cooking to taste and add the salt.

3 quarts (2.75 l) water
4 tablespoons olive oil
1 pound (450 g) zucchini, cut
    into ½-inch (1.5-cm) dice
4 garlic cloves, finely chopped
1 tablespoon chopped
    fresh mint
1 tablespoon chopped
    fresh basil
1 tablespoon chopped
    fresh Italian parsley
¼ teaspoon red pepper flakes
⅛ teaspoon saffron powder
    or turmeric
1 pound (450 g) small peeled
    shrimp (50-60 count),
    preferably rock shrimp
¼ cup dry white wine
1 cup Chicken Stock
    (see page 225)
¾ teaspoon salt
¼ teaspoon black pepper
1 pound (450 g) pasta -
    tortiglioni, rigatoni
    or penne rigate
4 tablespoons freshly grated
    Parmigiano Reggiano
    cheese
1 tablespoon butter (optional)

Bring the water to a boil in a large pot. Heat the olive oil in a large sauté pan set on high heat until sizzling, about 2 minutes. Add the zucchini and cook until it begins to brown, about 1 minute. Add the garlic, mint, basil, parsley, red pepper flakes, saffron or turmeric and shrimp and cook until the shrimp begins to turn pink, about 2 minutes. Pour in the wine and boil until reduced by half, about 2 minutes. Remove the pan from the heat. Transfer the shrimp to a bowl and set aside.

Return the pan of zucchini to medium-high heat, add the chicken stock, salt and pepper and bring to a boil. Reduce the heat to medium and simmer for 5-7 minutes. While the sauce is simmering, add the pasta to the boiling water and cook until just tender. Return the shrimp to the sauce to heat through.

Drain the cooked pasta and return it to the pot. Pour the sauce over the pasta and cook over medium heat for 3 minutes, stirring constantly. Stir in the cheese and the butter, if you wish. The pasta is ready to serve.

Wine Suggestion - Riesling

Pasta with Tuna and Asparagus

This is a very simple and colorful dinner. The lemon zest and capers bring out the tuna's flavor, while the pine nuts give it a great crunchy bite.

Bring the water to a boil in a large pot. Heat the olive oil in a large sauté pan set on high heat until sizzling, about 2 minutes. Cook the asparagus, pine nuts, sun-dried tomatoes, shallots, red pepper flakes, garlic, lemon zest and capers until the shallots soften and the garlic begins to brown, about 2-3 minutes. Pour in the wine and boil until reduced by half, about 2 minutes. Add the tuna, chicken stock, salt, pepper and lemon juice. Bring to a boil, reduce the heat to medium and cook for 4-5 minutes.

Cook the pasta in the boiling water until just tender. Drain the pasta well and return it to the pot. Pour the sauce over the pasta, sprinkle with the parsley and cook over medium heat for 3 minutes, stirring constantly. Remove from the heat, stir in the cheese and serve.

Wine Suggestion - Semillon

3 quarts (2.75 l) water

1 pound (450 g) pasta - penne rigate, rigatoni or tortiglioni

4 tablespoons olive oil

1 pound (450 g) asparagus, cut into 1-inch (2.5-cm) pieces

4 tablespoons pine nuts

4 tablespoons chopped oil-packed sun-dried tomatoes

¼ cup finely diced shallots or white onion

¼ teaspoon red pepper flakes

4 garlic cloves, thickly sliced

2 teaspoons grated lemon zest

4 tablespoons drained capers

¼ cup dry white wine

1 (6½-ounce) (190-g) can water-packed tuna, drained and flaked

¼ cup Chicken Stock (see page 225)

¾ teaspoon salt

¼ teaspoon black pepper

¼ cup lemon juice

3 tablespoons chopped fresh Italian parsley

¼ cup freshly grated Parmigiano Reggiano cheese

Paella Valenciana

This has been a popular Spanish classic for hundreds of years and is a great way to impress a crowd. You should note that paella requires a bit more time, effort and money than usual. Have all the ingredients ready to go once you start the cooking process. Read the directions carefully a few times and your efforts will be very well spent. (Illustrated in this section.)

1 teaspoon salt

¾ teaspoon black pepper

1 pound (450 g) chicken thighs, skin removed, boned and cut into quarters

3 tablespoons olive oil

½ pound (225 g) chorizo sausage or hot Italian link sausage, cut into ½-inch (1.5-cm) rounds

12 large shrimp (13-15 count), shelled and deveined

½ pound (225 g) thick-sliced bacon, cut into 1-inch (2.5-cm) pieces

6 garlic cloves, thickly sliced

¼ teaspoon red pepper flakes

2 bay leaves

2 tablespoons chopped fresh Italian parsley

2 teaspoons thyme

(continued)

Preheat the oven to 450° F (230° C). Place a large (4-quart) (3.75-l) casserole dish in the oven to preheat. Sprinkle ¼ teaspoon each of the salt and pepper on the chicken thighs. Heat 1 tablespoon of the olive oil in a large sauté pan set on high heat until sizzling, about 2 minutes. Cook the chicken thighs until well browned, about 2 minutes on each side. Remove to a bowl and set aside.

Add 1 tablespoon of the olive oil to the same pan and cook the sausage over high heat until browned, about 1-2 minutes. With a slotted spoon, remove to the same bowl with the chicken.

Add the remaining 1 tablespoon of olive oil to the pan and cook the shrimp over high heat until they begin to turn pink, about 1-2 minutes. Don't overcook the shrimp as it will continue to cook in the paella. With a slotted spoon, remove to a small bowl and set aside.

In the same pan, cook the bacon for 2-3 minutes, until it begins to brown and release some of its fat. Add the garlic, red pepper flakes, bay leaves, parsley, thyme, onion and bell pepper. Cook for 3-4 minutes, until the onion becomes translucent. Add the wine, clam juice, tomato sauce, saffron or turmeric, rice and the remaining salt and pepper. Cook for 3 minutes, stirring, until the rice begins to absorb some of the liquid.

Remove the heated casserole dish from the oven. Transfer the bubbling rice mixture from the pan to the casserole dish and stir in the chicken stock. Add the reserved browned chicken and sausage and mix well. Cover with a lid or aluminum foil and bake for 20 minutes, until the rice has absorbed all the liquid. Remove from the oven and stir in the reserved shrimp. Arrange the clams and mussels on top of the rice. Cover the casserole dish and return to the oven for 10 minutes longer, until the clams and mussels have opened. Discard any that don't.

Bring the casserole dish to the table so everyone can serve themselves.

Wine Suggestion - Merlot

1 onion, chopped

1 red bell pepper, cut into quarters lengthwise then cut into ½-inch (1.5-cm) slices crosswise

1 cup white wine

1 cup clam juice

1 cup Tomato Sauce (see page 222)

⅛ teaspoon saffron powder or turmeric

2½ cups converted long-grain rice

2 cups Chicken Stock (see page 225)

24 clams, cleaned

24 mussels, cleaned and de-bearded

Risotto with Peas

As you might know from watching my television series, creamy risotto dishes are one of my favorites. This is a very traditional Italian version, quite warm and comforting. I think the peas provide perfect punch.

6 cups Vegetable or Chicken Stock (see page 223 or 225)

2 tablespoons butter

2 tablespoons olive oil

1 onion, finely chopped

2 garlic cloves, chopped

3 cups arborio rice

3 cups frozen peas

1 cup dry white wine

½ teaspoon salt

¼ teaspoon black pepper

¼ head iceberg lettuce, cut into very thin strips (chiffonade)

2 tablespoons whipping cream (optional)

½ cup freshly grated Parmigiano Reggiano cheese

3 tablespoons chopped fresh Italian parsley

Bring the vegetable or chicken stock to a boil in a large covered saucepan. Reduce the heat to low and simmer until needed.

In a 4-quart (3.75-l) saucepan set on medium heat, cook the butter and olive oil until sizzling, about 2 minutes. Add the onion and cook for 2 minutes. Reduce the heat to low, add the garlic and cook for 4 minutes. Stir in the rice and peas and mix well. Raise the heat to medium-high and add the wine, salt and pepper, cooking until the wine is completely absorbed, about 2 minutes.

Add 3 cups of the simmering stock, stir well and bring to a boil for 2 minutes. Reduce the heat to low, cover, and let the rice cook, undisturbed, for 15 minutes. Uncover the saucepan and stir. Don't worry if it's dry. Raise the heat to medium, add the lettuce and ½ cup of the simmering stock, stirring continuously until all the stock is absorbed. Continue adding the stock ½ cup at a time, stirring continuously, until the rice is cooked, about 5-8 minutes. Taste the rice with each addition of the stock. It's perfectly cooked when the rice is tender to the bite. Don't worry if there is additional stock left.

Remove the pan from the heat, add a final ½ cup of stock, the cream, if you wish, the cheese and parsley and mix well. Let the risotto rest for 3 minutes. Serve while still piping hot.

Wine Suggestion - Sauvignon Blanc

You must reflect carefully beforehand
with whom you are to eat and drink,
rather than what you are to eat and drink.
For a dinner of meats without the company of a friend
is like the life of a lion or a wolf.

EPICURUS (342-270 B.C.)

ENTRÉES

A Little Big Dinner

My brother, Mario, and I both came to America to attend Arizona State University in Tempe. In our first year there together we shared a little bachelor's pad where I, as the elder son, took on the role of my brother's keeper - which included feeding him well. At the time, my culinary repertoire was pretty limited, but we had been raised in a family of cooks whose lessons I had absorbed almost unconsciously over the years.

Academically, I was immersed in international marketing, but at home - in our modest apartment kitchen - I felt like a chemistry major as I experimented day and night. I confess that the first real skill I perfected in that kitchen was dishwashing which, incidentally, came in much handier than I'd expected when I eventually decided to go into the food business full time.

Even though my culinary exploits were not always successful, I had the spirit of a bull and I was absolutely determined to succeed! One of my early attempts at "gourmet" cooking was trying to reproduce a recipe from my maternal grandmother, Nonna Adele. Grilled Polenta with Mushroom Sauce is a simple dish in which a glistening mushroom sauce falls over smoky polenta like a velvet comforter. I am sure that she would be embarrassed to hear her peasant fare so loftily described, but still ... Pretty soon I was able to concoct a reasonable facsimile of her dish, and the version that I've included in this book is the result of many subsequent refinements - and a few tips from Nonna Adele.

From there, I went on to try my hand at more sophisticated dishes like Chicken with Garlic Sauce, in which the meat is cooked to a golden amber color and dressed with a sumptuous sauce, redolent with garlic. It was motivation enough to keep cooking, just to see my often moody brother looking so contented.

Still, we were two homesick lads in need of hugs from Mom and a few words of wisdom from Dad, so their impending visit for the holidays was much anticipated. And, of course, I was eager to show off my newly honed kitchen skills by preparing a welcoming feast that I hoped would find an important place in the annals of Stellino family history!

My father's favorite meat was lamb and my mother's favorite herb was rosemary, so I decided to make a dish inspired by one that I had tried in a little French restaurant in Phoenix - a rack of lamb with mustard, garlic and rosemary. Without a recipe to follow, the real challenge for me was to work out the proportions of spices and herbs, not to mention the cooking time and so forth. I made a quick trip to the local library where I studied recipe after recipe in search of what I needed to know. Still, I ended up having to experiment many times on Mario and his soccer buddies. There were few complaints since the food was abundant and, of course, free. I must admit that there were some failures, but I was caught up in the spirit of the venture and discovered in myself a real passion for the cooking business.

With Mario as my reluctant sous chef, the pieces did eventually all come together and, on the big day, we set the table with my mother's favorite yellow roses, popped the rack of lamb into the oven and set off to the airport to pick up our parents.

Mom and Dad arrived tired from the long trip but excited to be with us and hear our tall tales of life in America. As happy as I was to see them, I was eager to get home to the big banquet.

This is a story, I'm happy to report, with no disasters ... because I know that you're expecting to hear about some kitchen catastrophe or other. Instead, from the moment we walked through the door, the gorgeous aroma of the lamb carried us straight to the kitchen. At the dinner table, with the family joined together after a long absence, we relished our sumptuous feast.

That night is memorable for us all - the hugs, the laughter, the sharing of love ... and the food. I hope that all the dishes that I offer you in this book will be enjoyed in the company of friends and family to make every occasion as special as the Stellinos' reunion. And remember, there is not an ingredient that matters more than a little passion from your heart!

The discovery of a new dish
does more for the happiness of mankind
than the discovery of a star.

BRILLAT-SAVARIN

Asparagus Frittata

This recipe, a gorgeous golden egg pie, with tender asparagus pieces, mixes two culinary styles: the Italian egg frittata and the Spanish tortilla. It's perfect for breakfast, but would make a satisfying light dinner with something like my Mushroom Salad (page 55) and a large piece of hearty bread.

4 tablespoons olive oil

1 pound (450 g) thin-stalked
    asparagus, cut into 1-inch
    (2.5-cm) pieces*

½ bunch (5 to 6) green onions
    including 2 inches (5 cm)
    of the green parts, thinly
    sliced

4 garlic cloves, finely chopped

¼ teaspoon red pepper flakes

1 tablespoon chopped fresh
    basil or 1 teaspoon dried

1 tablespoon chopped
    fresh Italian parsley

2 tablespoons chopped
    fresh mint

8 eggs

¾ teaspoon salt

¼ teaspoon black pepper

½ cup freshly grated
    Pecorino Romano cheese

Preheat the oven to 350° F (180° C). Heat 2 tablespoons of the olive oil in a large (12-inch) (30-cm) ovenproof nonstick sauté pan set on medium-high heat until it sizzles, about 2 minutes. Cook the asparagus and green onions until the asparagus begins to brown, about 1½ minutes. Add the garlic, red pepper flakes, basil, parsley and mint and cook for 2 minutes. Remove from the heat.

In a large bowl, beat the eggs, salt, pepper and cheese until well mixed. Stir in the asparagus mixture.

Heat the remaining olive oil in the same sauté pan set on medium-high heat until sizzling, about 2 minutes. Add the egg mixture and cook for 2 minutes. Transfer the omelette to the oven and cook for 12 minutes. Remove from the oven and flip the omelette over in the pan to cook the other side. The easiest way to do this is to place a large plate over the sauté pan. Put your hand on top of the plate and turn the pan over. Slide the omelette, which is now cooked-side-up, from the plate into the sauté pan and cook for an additional 12 minutes in the oven. Transfer from the pan to a serving plate and cut into wedges. Serve warm or refrigerate overnight for the flavors to mature. Bring to room temperature before serving.

Note: If using thick-stalked asparagus, cut the stalks in half lengthwise, before cutting into 1-inch (2.5-cm) pieces.

Wine Suggestion - Semillon-Chardonnay

Grilled Polenta with Mushroom Sauce

⌄

SERVES 4

Slightly sweet and extremely satisfying, polenta is a Mediterranean staple that should be served more often in other parts of the world. In this recipe, the savory polenta corn cake is topped with a cheese sauce bursting with mushrooms. The optional truffle oil is definitely decadent, but worth the expense for a special occasion.

Mix the mushrooms, garlic and parsley together in a medium bowl. Cover with plastic wrap and refrigerate for 1 hour to let the flavors mingle.

Cook the polenta as directed and spread it in a greased 9-inch (23-cm) square baking dish. Set the polenta aside for at least 30 minutes, until firm. Cut into 4 squares and then cut each square in half from corner to corner to make 2 triangles. Set aside.

Heat the butter and red pepper flakes in a large sauté pan set on high heat, until the butter is melted and sizzling, about 1 minute. Add the mushroom mixture and cook until the mushrooms are limp and have released their juices, about 4-5 minutes. Stir in the wine and boil until reduced by half, about 2-3 minutes. Add the cream, vegetable or chicken stock, salt and pepper and bring to a boil. Stir in the cream cheese and cook until it has completely melted. Continue to cook over high heat until the sauce has thickened enough to coat the back of a spoon, about 4-5 minutes. Remove from the heat and add the Parmigiano and Swiss cheeses, stirring until completely melted. Set aside and cover to keep warm.

Grill, sauté or broil the polenta triangles according to the directions on page 231, until lightly browned. To serve, place 2 polenta triangles on each dish. Stir the truffle oil into the sauce, if you wish, before spooning it over the polenta.

Wine Suggestion - Sauvignon Blanc

¾ pound (350 g) mushrooms, sliced

4 garlic cloves, chopped

2 tablespoons chopped fresh Italian parsley

1 recipe Polenta (see page 231) or half of a (13-ounce) (375-g) package instant polenta

3 tablespoons butter

¼ teaspoon red pepper flakes

½ cup white wine

¼ cup whipping cream

1 cup Vegetable or Chicken Stock (see page 223 or 225)

¼ teaspoon salt

½ teaspoon black pepper

¼ cup cream cheese

¼ cup freshly grated Parmigiano Reggiano cheese

½ cup shredded Swiss cheese

2 teaspoons truffle oil (optional)

Eggplant Parmesan

⌄

SERVES 4

Some recipes leap across borders to international fame, like this Italian classic. Tender layers of eggplant, cheese and tomato sauce are baked together into a rich, earthy casserole - a very satisfying vegetable main dish.

2 (1½-pound) (700-g)
  eggplants, sliced ½ inch
  (1.5 cm) thick

1½ teaspoons salt

3 tablespoons olive oil

1¼ cups Tomato Sauce
  (see page 222)

20 whole basil leaves

1½ cups shredded
  mozzarella cheese

1 cup freshly grated
  Parmigiano Reggiano
  cheese

½ teaspoon black pepper

Early in the day of serving, sprinkle the eggplant slices with the salt and lay the slices on top of one another in a large colander. Place a dish on top and weight it down (a large can of tomatoes works well). Drain for 20 minutes. Dry the eggplant slices with paper towels.

Preheat the oven to 425° F (220° C). Brush a nonstick baking sheet with the olive oil. Brush both sides of the eggplant slices with the olive oil, lay in a single layer on the prepared sheet and cook for 25 minutes, until lightly browned. Set aside until cool enough to handle.

Preheat the oven to 400° F (200° C). Spread ¼ cup of the tomato sauce over the bottom of a 9 x 13-inch (23 x 33-cm) baking dish. Lay one-third of the eggplant slices over the tomato sauce. Spread ¼ cup of tomato sauce over the eggplant slices. Lay 10 of the basil leaves evenly over the tomato sauce, sprinkle with ½ cup of the mozzarella cheese, ¼ cup of the Parmigiano Reggiano cheese and ¼ teaspoon of the black pepper. Repeat these layers once more, beginning with the eggplant slices. For the final layer, top with the remaining one-third of the eggplant slices, the remaining ½ cup of tomato sauce, the remaining ½ cup of mozzarella cheese and the remaining ½ cup of Parmigiano Reggiano cheese. (The casserole can prepared ahead to this point and refrigerated, covered.) Bake the casserole, uncovered, for 30-35 minutes, until the sides are bubbling and the top is golden brown. (If the casserole was refrigerated before baking, cook for 45-50 minutes.) Let the casserole rest for 10 minutes before cutting into squares for serving.

Wine Suggestion - Merlot

Stuffed Eggplant Rolls

My Sicilian childhood includes so many wonderful meals centered around eggplant. I love the unusual presentation: a savory stuffing enclosed in an eggplant roll. You can prepare the rolls ahead of time and refrigerate until ready to bake with the sauce.

Trim the ends of the eggplants and cut lengthwise into ¼-inch (6-mm) slices. Discard the outer slices. There should be about 8 usable slices from each eggplant. Sprinkle the slices with the salt and lay on top of one another in a large colander. Place a dish on top and weight it down with a heavy object (a large can of tomatoes works well). Drain for 20 minutes. Pat dry with paper towels.

Preheat the oven to 425° F (220° C). Brush a nonstick baking pan and both sides of the eggplant slices with 3 tablespoons of the olive oil. Roast for 25 minutes, until lightly browned. Set aside.

Heat the remaining olive oil in a large sauté pan set on medium-high heat until sizzling, about 2 minutes. Cook the garlic, mushrooms, pepper, basil and ham until the mushrooms have released their juices, about 3-4 minutes. Stir in the wine and boil until reduced by half, about 3-4 minutes. Transfer the mixture to a bowl and mix in the bread crumbs and ¼ cup of the Romano cheese. The stuffing should be on the drier side. If too moist, add more bread crumbs.

Preheat the oven to 400° F (200° C). Place 1-2 tablespoons of the filling at the large end of the eggplant slices. Roll the eggplant slices up, enclosing the stuffing. Set aside.

Pour the chicken stock and tomato sauce into a 9 x 13-inch (23 x 33-cm) baking dish, stirring to mix. Place the eggplant rolls in the sauce and top with the mozzarella cheese and the remaining Romano cheese. Bake for 30 minutes, until the cheese is brown and the sauce is bubbling. Serve 2-3 rolls per person.

2 (1-pound) (450-g) eggplants

¼ teaspoon salt

5 tablespoons olive oil

4 garlic cloves, chopped

¾ pound (350 g) button mushrooms, quartered

¼ teaspoon black pepper

4 tablespoons chopped fresh basil

1 cup chopped ham

½ cup white wine

½ cup Italian Bread Crumbs (see page 230)

½ cup freshly grated Pecorino Romano cheese

½ cup Chicken Stock (see page 225)

1 cup Tomato Sauce (see page 222)

1 cup shredded mozzarella cheese

Wine Suggestion - Cabernet Sauvignon

Spinach and Cheese Pie

One of the great Greek flavor partnerships is spinach and feta cheese. I've added an Italian twist with the ricotta cheese, which provides a great deal of creaminess. And if you've never used frozen puff pastry dough before, you'll be amazed how easy it is to use for the buttery top crust.

3 tablespoons olive oil

1 large onion, finely chopped

4 garlic cloves, finely chopped

¼ teaspoon red pepper flakes

¼ teaspoon ground cinnamon

⅛ teaspoon ground nutmeg

¼ teaspoon salt

¼ teaspoon black pepper

2 (10-ounce) (300-g) packages frozen chopped spinach, thawed and squeezed to remove excess moisture

1 cup ricotta cheese

2½ cups (¾ pound) (350 g) crumbled feta cheese

½ cup freshly grated Pecorino Romano cheese

3 eggs

1 sheet frozen puff pastry, thawed

Preheat the oven to 400° F (200° C). Grease a 9 x 13-inch (23 x 33-cm) baking dish. Heat the olive oil in a large sauté pan set on high heat until sizzling, about 2 minutes. Cook the onion for 1 minute, then add the garlic, red pepper flakes, cinnamon, nutmeg, salt and pepper. Cook for 2-3 minutes longer, until the onion begins to brown. Transfer the cooked onions to a large bowl. Stir in the spinach, ricotta, feta, Romano and 2 of the eggs. Pour the mixture into the prepared baking dish.

Roll out the sheet of puff pastry on a lightly floured board until large enough to cover the spinach filling. Lay the puff pastry over the spinach, tucking the edges under if there is a little excess on the sides. Lightly score the top of the puff pastry into 8 squares, being careful not to cut all the way through. (Scoring the puff pastry before cooking will ensure a neater appearance when the pie is served.) Beat the remaining egg in a small bowl and brush over the top of the pastry. Cover tightly with foil and bake for 30 minutes. Increase the temperature to 425° F (220° C), remove the foil and bake for an additional 15 minutes. Remove from the oven and cool for 15 minutes. Cut the squares on the scored lines and serve.

Cook's Tip

For a tasty variation on the basic spinach pie, stir ½ cup sliced, pitted California black olives into the spinach mixture before it is spooned into the baking dish.

Wine Suggestion - Semillon

Spanish Chicken with Almond Sauce

Any dish that fills your house with a perfume like this one will be cooked again and again, but couple that quality with the fact that this dinner also tastes great! I use boneless chicken breasts with skin for this recipe, which gives you the tender flesh and a crispy skin. If you don't know how to cut these from a whole chicken, just ask your butcher to do it while you're at the store.

For the Spanish Chicken, preheat the oven to 325° F (170° C). Combine the flour, nutmeg, cinnamon, salt and pepper on a large plate. Coat the chicken breasts with the flour mixture, patting off the excess. Heat the olive oil in a large sauté pan set on medium-high heat until sizzling, about 2 minutes. Add the chicken breasts, skin-side-down, and cook for 4 minutes on each side. Transfer the breasts to a baking dish and bake for 10-15 minutes.

While the breasts are baking, prepare the Almond Sauce. Add the olive oil to the same pan set on medium-high heat and cook until sizzling, about 1 minute. Add the garlic, onion, cinnamon, nutmeg, bay leaf and almonds. Cook until the onion softens and the garlic begins to brown, about 3 minutes. Stir in the sherry or wine and boil until reduced by half, about 1-2 minutes. Add the chicken stock and saffron or turmeric, bring to a boil and cook until reduced by half, about 7-8 minutes. Remove the pan from the heat and quickly stir in the egg yolk to thicken. Don't return the pan to the heat or the yolk will break up. There is enough heat in the sauce to cook the yolk and thicken the sauce.

To serve, place the breasts on serving plates, top with the sauce and a sprinkle of the chopped parsley.

Wine Suggestion - Riesling

SPANISH CHICKEN
2 tablespoons flour
¼ teaspoon nutmeg
¼ teaspoon cinnamon
¾ teaspoon salt
½ teaspoon black pepper
4 boneless chicken breasts, with skin on
2 tablespoons olive oil

ALMOND SAUCE
1 tablespoon olive oil
4 garlic cloves, thickly sliced
½ onion, chopped
½ teaspoon cinnamon
½ teaspoon nutmeg
1 bay leaf
⅓ cup sliced almonds
¼ cup dry sherry or white wine
1 cup Chicken Stock (see page 225)
⅛ teaspoon saffron powder or turmeric
1 egg yolk, beaten
3 tablespoons chopped fresh Italian parsley

Chicken with Garlic Sauce

A truly outstanding dish! This is my simplified version of the French classic, Chicken with 40 Cloves of Garlic. Tender chicken breasts are subtly seasoned with herbs and baked so they come out of the oven with a crispy skin. The sauce is a garlic lover's dream, prepared easily on the stove top while the chicken bakes. It will fill your home (and maybe your neighbor's, as well) with an irresistible fragrance.

2 tablespoons flour

1½ teaspoons sage

1½ teaspoons rosemary

¾ teaspoon salt

½ teaspoon black pepper

4 (6-ounce) (175-g) boneless chicken breasts, with skin on (see Cook's Tip)

3 tablespoons olive oil

20 garlic cloves, cut in half lengthwise

¼ teaspoon red pepper flakes

½ white onion, chopped

¼ cup white wine

1¼ cups Chicken Stock (see page 225)

1 tablespoon soft butter mixed with 1 tablespoon flour (see Cook's Tip)

3 tablespoons chopped fresh Italian parsley

Preheat the oven to 325°F (170°C). Combine the flour, sage, rosemary, salt and pepper on a plate. Dredge the chicken breasts in the flour mixture, shaking off the excess flour. Heat 2 tablespoons of the olive oil in a large sauté pan set on medium-high heat until sizzling, about 2 minutes. Add the chicken breasts to the pan, skin-side-down, and cook for 4 minutes on each side. Transfer to a baking dish, skin-side-up, and cook for 10-15 minutes in the preheated oven.

While the chicken is baking, add the remaining olive oil to the sauté pan used for browning the chicken and heat over medium-high heat until sizzling, about 1 minute. Add the garlic, red pepper flakes and onion and cook until the onion softens and the garlic begins to brown, about 3 minutes. Stir the wine into the pan, scraping up any brown bits from the bottom. Boil the wine until reduced by half, about 2-3 minutes. Add the chicken stock and boil until reduced by half, about 7-8 minutes. Remove the pan from the heat and whisk in the butter-flour mixture, stirring until it has melted completely. Return the pan to the heat and boil for a minute, until the sauce thickens. Keep warm until ready to serve.

To serve, place the chicken breasts on serving plates, top with the sauce and a sprinkle of the chopped parsley.

Cook's Tip

Chicken Breasts - Boneless chicken breasts with the skin on are normally not available at your grocery. You'll have to purchase bone-in chicken breasts and bone them at home, or ask your butcher to do it. I like leaving the skin on because it gives the breast a nice golden finish, as well as ensuring a more moist finished product. Boneless, skinless chicken breasts can be used, but the finished product may be drier. Be careful not to overcook them. If you use breasts with the bone in, the cooking time will be longer.

Thickening Sauces - The butter-flour paste used in this recipe, known as *beurre manié*, is an ideal last minute thickener for sauces. For each cup of sauce, mix 1 tablespoon each of flour and soft butter to a smooth paste with a spoon or rubber spatula. This mixture can be made ahead and refrigerated until needed.

To make the sauce, remove the pan of hot liquid to be thickened from the heat and stir in the butter-flour paste until completely melted. Return the pan to the heat and boil briefly, until thickened.

Wine Suggestion - Cabernet Franc

This dish is the ultimate proof that there is no such thing as too much garlic. The recipe will not overpower your senses, rather it will seduce you into a sweet gourmand bliss.

Chicken Cordon Bleu

⌄

SERVES 4

It's funny but true how simple additions to the humble chicken breast make it not just a "delicious dinner," but something richly indulgent, to celebrate your most special moments. My rendition of this French classic will convince you of the truth of this statement. Enjoy it soon.

4 boneless chicken breasts

4 thin slices honey-glazed ham

4 thin slices Swiss cheese

½ teaspoon salt

½ teaspoon black pepper

2 tablespoons flour

3 eggs, beaten

1½ cups plain bread crumbs

2 tablespoons butter

3 tablespoons olive oil

1 tablespoon chopped garlic

⅛ teaspoon red pepper flakes

¼ cup chopped shallots

½ pound (225 g) mushrooms,
   sliced

¼ cup sparkling or white wine

1½ cups Chicken Stock
   (see page 225)

1 tablespoon soft butter mixed
   with 1 tablespoon flour

2 tablespoons chopped fresh
   Italian parsley

Cut a deep pocket on the side of each chicken breast almost to the edge of the back of the breast, but being careful not to slice through. Stuff each breast with a slice of the ham and the cheese. Mix together ¼ teaspoon of the salt, ¼ teaspoon of the pepper and the 2 tablespoons of flour. Coat the chicken breasts with the seasoned flour, patting off the excess. Dip the floured breasts in the beaten eggs and then roll them in the bread crumbs. Repeat this once more with each breast.

Preheat the oven to 350° F (180° C). Heat the butter and 2 tablespoons of the olive oil in a large sauté pan set on medium-high heat until it begins sizzling and the butter starts to brown, about 2 minutes. Cook the breasts 2 at a time to get an even browning and a golden crust, about 2 minutes on each side. Place the browned breasts on a baking sheet and bake in the oven for 15 minutes.

While the chicken bakes, make the sauce. Add the remaining olive oil to the pan in which the chicken breasts were cooked and place over high heat. Add the garlic, red pepper flakes, shallots and mushrooms and cook for 2 minutes. Stir in the wine and boil until reduced by half, about 1-2 minutes. Add the chicken stock and the remaining salt and pepper and boil until the stock is slightly thickened, about 7 minutes. Remove the pan from the heat and stir in the butter-flour mixture to thicken the sauce. When the chicken is ready, transfer it to serving dishes, top with the sauce and a sprinkle of the chopped parsley.

Wine Suggestion - Pinot Noir

Chicken Scallopini with Ham and Asparagus

When sweet honey ham and tender asparagus pieces are served with meltingly tender chicken breast slices, the result is irresistible! The most important step is to pre-pound the meat slices to the proper thickness. This can be done a day ahead of time. Just put the pieces between layers of plastic wrap or wax paper and store in the refrigerator. (Illustrated in this section.)

Remove the chicken tenderloin, the thin tapering piece of meat on the lower edge of the breast, from each breast half and freeze for another use. Slice each chicken breast into 3 pieces, widthwise across the grain. Pound the slices lightly between 2 pieces of plastic wrap to a thickness of ¼ inch (6 mm). Sprinkle both sides of the chicken pieces with ¼ teaspoon of the salt, ¼ teaspoon of the pepper and dust with the flour, shaking off any excess.

Heat 3 tablespoons of the olive oil and 1 tablespoon of the butter in a large sauté pan set on high heat until the olive oil starts to sizzle, about 2 minutes. Add the prepared chicken slices in one layer and cook 1 minute on each side, until lightly browned. You may need to brown the chicken in 2 batches depending on the size of the pan. Transfer the chicken to a plate and set aside.

Add the remaining olive oil to the same pan set on high heat. Cook the garlic, red pepper flakes, thyme, asparagus and ham for 1 minute, stirring well. Pour in the wine and boil until reduced by half, about 1-2 minutes. Stir in the chicken stock and the remaining salt and pepper and bring to a boil. Cook for 1 minute. Return the browned chicken to the pan to reheat for 1 minute. Remove the pan from the heat and transfer the chicken to serving dishes. Stir the remaining butter into the sauce to thicken. Top the chicken with the sauce and serve.

Wine Suggestion - Semillon-Chardonnay

4 (6- to 8-ounce) (175- to 225-g) boneless chicken breasts

½ teaspoon salt

½ teaspoon black pepper

4 tablespoons flour

4 tablespoons olive oil

4 tablespoons cold butter

3 garlic cloves, thickly sliced

⅛ teaspoon red pepper flakes

1 teaspoon thyme

½ pound (225 g) asparagus cut into ¼-inch (6-mm) pieces (If spears are fat, cut in half lengthwise before cutting into pieces.)

½ cup honey-glazed ham, cut into small dice

½ cup white wine

½ cup Chicken Stock (see page 225)

Stuffed Chicken Rolls with Mushroom Sauce

SERVES 8

Here's your solution to an impressive dish that can be prepared ahead for your dinner guests! Savory vegetable stuffing is rolled up inside chicken breasts that are baked in a brandy-spiked mushroom sauce. Make them a day in advance and just keep them in the refrigerator. You can brown and bake them quickly before serving.

8 (6- to 8-ounce) (175- to 225-g) boneless chicken breasts

½ recipe Vegetarian Stuffing (see page 233)

3 tablespoons flour

3 tablespoons olive oil

2 tablespoons butter

6 garlic cloves, thickly sliced

½ cup finely chopped shallots or white onion

¾ pound (350 g) button mushrooms, quartered

½ cup brandy

2 cups Chicken Stock (see page 225)

2 tablespoons chopped fresh Italian parsley

1 tablespoon soft butter mixed with 1 tablespoon flour (optional)

Remove the chicken tenderloin, the thin tapering piece of meat on the lower edge of the breast, from each breast half and freeze for another use. Slice each chicken breast into 3 pieces, widthwise across the grain. Pound the slices lightly between 2 pieces of plastic wrap to a thickness of ¼ inch (6 mm). Place one-eighth of the stuffing down the center of each breast. Fold the short sides of the breast over the filling and the long sides over the short sides. Secure the rolls with 1 or 2 toothpicks and then roll in the flour, shaking off any excess.

Heat the olive oil in a large sauté pan set on medium-high heat until sizzling, about 2 minutes. Brown the chicken rolls in 2 batches, seam-side-down, for 3-4 minutes on each side. Transfer to a plate and set aside.

Discard any oil left in the pan. Melt the butter in the same pan set on high heat. Add the garlic, shallots or onion and mushrooms, cooking for 2-3 minutes, until the shallots become translucent and the mushrooms begin to soften and brown. Add the brandy and boil until reduced by half, about 1-2 minutes. Stir in the chicken stock and bring to a boil. Reduce for 7 minutes, until the stock is slightly thickened.

Place the reserved chicken rolls in the sauce to reheat for about 1 minute on each side. Transfer the chicken rolls to a serving dish. Remove the pan from the heat and add the chopped parsley and the butter-flour paste to the sauce, if you wish, stirring until the paste is completely melted. Return the pan to the heat for 1 minute to thicken. Top the breasts with the sauce and serve.

Wine Suggestion - Sauvignon Blanc

Pesto Marinated Chicken Breasts

⌄

SERVES 4

This is probably one of the tastiest chicken recipes you'll ever make. I think you'll find that the squeeze of lemon juice really brings out a bright color from the basil and provides a refreshing balance to the rich sauce. It is a foolproof method to get juicy tender chicken breasts.

The day before serving, mix the pesto with the lemon juice and salt. Pour into an 8 x 8-inch (20 x 20-cm) baking dish or medium bowl. Put the breasts in the marinade and toss to coat completely. Cover and refrigerate overnight or for at least 6 hours.

Preheat the oven to 350°F (180°C). Place the breasts on a baking sheet and pour the extra marinade over them. Bake for 20 minutes. Serve hot, at room temperature or cold for a picnic.

½ cup Pesto Sauce
(see page 82)

¼ cup fresh lemon juice

½ teaspoon salt

4 (6- to 8-ounce) (175- to 225-g) boneless chicken breasts

Cook's Tip

This marinade is also marvelous on fish fillets. Simply substitute 4 (6- to 8-ounce) (175- to 225-g) halibut fillets. Marinate the fillets for 2 hours. Preheat the oven to 400°F (200°C). Place the fillets on a baking sheet, pour on the marinade and bake for 10-15 minutes, depending on the thickness. Cook ¾-inch (2-cm) fillets for 10 minutes, larger ones for 15 minutes. Serve hot.

Wine Suggestion - Syrah

Moroccan Chicken with Olives

❖

SERVES 4

Your family and friends won't recognize chicken with this festive Moroccan sauce filled with spices, olives, and the fresh tang of lemon juice. Please remember to inhale deeply while cooking, for this dish has a pure Mediterranean perfume.

1½ teaspoons cumin

1½ teaspoons ginger

1½ teaspoons cinnamon

¼ teaspoon salt

½ teaspoon pepper

3 tablespoons flour

1 (3- to 4-pound) (1.4- to 1.8-kg) chicken, cut into pieces

3 tablespoons olive oil

4 garlic cloves, thickly sliced

¼ teaspoon red pepper flakes

1 white onion, chopped

2 bay leaves

½ cup pitted green olives, halved

½ cup pitted Greek or Sicilian black olives, halved (see Cook's Tip)

½ cup white wine

1½ cups Chicken Stock (see page 225)

⅛ teaspoon saffron powder or turmeric

3 tablespoons chopped fresh Italian parsley

3-4 tablespoons lemon juice (to taste)

Combine the cumin, ginger, cinnamon, salt, pepper and flour. Coat the chicken pieces with the flour mixture, shaking off any excess. Reserve the leftover flour mixture.

Heat the olive oil in a large sauté pan set on high heat until sizzling, about 2 minutes. Add the chicken pieces and cook for 3-4 minutes per side, until golden brown. Transfer the chicken to a bowl and set aside.

In the same pan set on medium-high heat, cook the garlic, red pepper flakes, onion, bay leaves and both olives, stirring occasionally. Cook until the onion is soft and the garlic is beginning to brown, about 3-4 minutes. Add the reserved flour mixture to the pan and cook for 1 minute. Stir in the wine and boil until reduced by half, about 1-2 minutes. Add the chicken stock, saffron or turmeric and the reserved browned chicken. Bring to a boil, reduce the heat to low and simmer for 15-20 minutes. Stir in the parsley and lemon juice just before serving.

Cook's Tip

If you are unable to find Greek or Sicilian black olives in your market, California black olives can be substituted. The flavors will not be as pronounced, but it's still a thoroughly enjoyable dish.

Wine Suggestion - Chardonnay

OPPOSITE: (TOP) TURKISH KEBABS (PAGES 136-137), (BOTTOM) RICE PILAF WITH CURRANTS AND PINE NUTS (PAGE 170).

Turkey Scallopini with Curry Sauce

SERVES 4

You won't believe the new personality that my North African curry sauce brings to the common turkey breast! If you're unable to find the whole turkey breast on its own, then ask your butcher to cut some for you. However, if it's easier, you can certainly do this with chicken. Just use the same amount and the pounding method from the Chicken Scallopini recipe (page 117).

Cut the turkey breasts across the grain (widthwise) into slices about ¾ inch (2 cm) thick. Lay the slices, cut-side-up, on a cutting board and lightly pound them between 2 pieces of plastic wrap to a thickness of ¼ inch (6 mm). Don't pound too energetically or the turkey slices will tear. Sprinkle the turkey with the salt, pepper and flour, shaking off any excess.

Heat 3 tablespoons of the olive oil and 1 tablespoon of the butter in a large sauté pan set on high heat until sizzling, about 2 minutes. Add the turkey slices in a single layer and cook for 1 minute on each side, until lightly browned. You will need to cook the slices in two to three batches. Remove to a plate and set aside.

Add the remaining olive oil to the same pan set on high heat. Cook the garlic, red pepper flakes, curry powder, shallots or onion and basil, stirring well, about 1 minute. Pour in the wine and boil until reduced by half, about 1-2 minutes. Stir in the chicken stock and parsley, bring to a boil and reduce the heat to a simmer. Return the browned turkey and any juices that have accumulated to the pan, along with the peas, simmering for 1 minute to heat the turkey and peas.

Remove the pan from the heat and transfer the turkey to a serving platter. Return the pan to the heat and stir the remaining 3 tablespoons of butter into the sauce to thicken. Top the turkey with the sauce and serve.

Wine Suggestion - Chardonnay

1¼ pounds (560 g) turkey breast
½ teaspoon salt
½ teaspoon black pepper
4 tablespoons flour
4 tablespoons olive oil
4 tablespoons cold unsalted butter
3 garlic cloves, thickly sliced
⅛ teaspoon red pepper flakes
2 teaspoons curry powder
¼ cup chopped shallots or white onion
1 tablespoon chopped fresh basil or 1 teaspoon dried
½ cup white wine
½ cup Chicken Stock (see page 225)
1 tablespoon chopped fresh Italian parsley
½ cup frozen peas, thawed

OPPOSITE: BEEF AND BELL PEPPER STEW (PAGE 130). PREVIOUS LEFT PAGE: GORGONZOLA PORK CHOPS (PAGE 124), GINGER-GLAZED CARROTS (PAGE 156). PREVIOUS RIGHT PAGE: CHICKEN SCALLOPINI WITH HAM AND ASPARAGUS (PAGE 117), ROMANO MASHED POTATOES (PAGE 164).

Moroccan Chicken and Almond Pie

Morocco's version of this global favorite potpie, is distinctly unique: a highly seasoned chicken and egg filling is topped with a sweet almond layer before being topped with a flaky phyllo dough crust and dusted with powdered sugar. While I have simplified the traditional preparation considerably, it is still a somewhat complex process. Read the directions carefully and have fun ... you'll love it!

ALMOND LAYER

1½ cups sliced almonds

3 tablespoons sugar

1 teaspoon cinnamon

CHICKEN FILLING

4 tablespoons butter

4 garlic cloves, chopped

2 onions, chopped

2 teaspoons cinnamon

2 teaspoons cumin

¼ teaspoon cayenne

2 teaspoons ginger

¼ teaspoon saffron powder
   or turmeric

¼ cup Chicken Stock
   (see page 225)

1½ pounds (700 g) boneless
   chicken breasts or
   a mixture of breasts
   and boneless thighs

(continued)

To prepare the Almond Layer, preheat the oven to 375° F (190° C). Toast the almonds on a baking sheet for 5-7 minutes, until golden brown. Cool the almonds and coarsely chop in a food processor or blender. Transfer to a medium bowl and stir in the sugar and cinnamon. Set aside.

To prepare the Chicken Filling, heat the butter in a large high-sided fry pan set on medium-high heat until sizzling, about 1-2 minutes. Add the garlic, onions, cinnamon, cumin, cayenne, ginger and saffron or turmeric and cook until the onions are translucent and their juices have been released and evaporated, about 10 minutes. Stir in the chicken stock and bring to a boil. Add the chicken, reduce the heat to medium, cover the pan and cook for 15-20 minutes, turning the chicken several times to ensure it cooks evenly. Remove the chicken breasts to a plate and cool.

Boil the cooking liquid over medium heat, stirring often, until reduced to 1 cup, about 8-10 minutes. The sauce will be dark and have a thick consistency. Set the pan of reduced sauce aside.

When the chicken has cooled enough to handle, cut the meat into 1-inch (2.5-cm) chunks or shred it. Add the diced chicken to the reduced sauce along with the salt, pepper, lemon juice and parsley, mixing well. Cook the mixture over medium heat. Stir in the eggs, using a spatula to stir and scrape the sides of the pan. Cook until soft curds form, about 5-7 minutes. The filling shouldn't be too dry or overly wet. Set aside.

To assemble the Chicken Pie, finish with the Phyllo Crust. Preheat the oven to 375°F (190°C). Brush a 12- to 14-inch (30- to 35-cm) round pizza pan with the butter. (If you don't have a round pizza pan, you can use a rectangular baking sheet. You'll need to arrange the phyllo sheets in a free-form circle to shape the pie.) Arrange 8 sheets of the phyllo in a pinwheel pattern on the pan, brushing each one with the butter first. The sheets should overlap and hang over the edge of the pan.

Spread the filling mixture evenly over the phyllo to the edge of the pan. Place 2 sheets of the phyllo over the filling and brush with the butter. Spread the almond mixture evenly over the phyllo to the edge of the pan. Fold the overhanging ends of the phyllo over the filling. You will get the best results by bringing up one sheet at a time. Lay 8 more buttered sheets of phyllo over the filling in an overlapping pinwheel pattern, just as you did on the bottom of the pan. Gently tuck the overhanging ends of the phyllo under the pie. Brush the remaining butter over the top.

Bake until the top is golden, about 20 minutes. Remove from the oven and pour off any excess butter. Invert a large plate or a large baking sheet with no sides over the pie. Holding firmly, turn the pie over onto the plate and then slide it back onto the pizza pan so the bottom is now facing up. Return to the oven and bake for 20 minutes. Remove from the oven and invert again so the original top is facing up. Return to the oven and bake for 5 minutes longer.

Remove the pie from the oven and slide onto a serving platter. Let it rest for 10-15 minutes. Dust the top with the powdered sugar and cinnamon, cut into wedges and serve warm.

Wine Suggestion - Gewürztraminer

1¼ teaspoons salt

½ teaspoon black pepper

¼ cup lemon juice

½ cup chopped fresh
　Italian parsley

8 eggs, lightly beaten

PHYLLO CRUST

8 tablespoons butter, melted

18 frozen phyllo sheets,
　thawed

4 tablespoons powdered sugar

1 teaspoon cinnamon

Gorgonzola Pork Chops

⌄

SERVES 4

You might already know that pork and apples make a perfect marriage, but the addition of the Gorgonzola cheese makes a "trinity!" Very easy and fast to make, you can also stuff the pork chops the night before and store them in the refrigerator. (Illustrated in this section.)

APPLE-STUFFED
PORK CHOPS

1 tablespoon butter

1 cup chopped peeled apple

1 teaspoon thyme

¼ cup crumbled
   Gorgonzola cheese

4 (8- to 10-ounce) (225- to
   300-g) pork chops, 1-1½
   inches (2.5-4 cm) thick

¼ teaspoon salt

¼ teaspoon black pepper

2 tablespoons olive oil

GORGONZOLA SAUCE

1½ teaspoons butter

2 garlic cloves, thickly sliced

¾ cup Chicken Stock
   (see page 225)

2 tablespoons whipping cream

½ cup crumbled
   Gorgonzola cheese

¼ teaspoon black pepper

1 tablespoon chopped fresh
   Italian parsley

For the Apple-Stuffed Pork Chops, melt the butter in a small sauté pan set on medium-high heat until sizzling, about 1-2 minutes. Add the apple and thyme and cook until soft and beginning to brown, about 3 minutes. Transfer the apples to a small bowl and stir in the Gorgonzola. Set aside to cool.

Insert a thin-bladed knife in the side of each chop and cut a pocket that's almost the same size as the chop. Fill each pocket with the cooled apple stuffing. Don't overstuff the pork chops, as excess stuffing will fall out during cooking when the pork chops shrink. Sprinkle the chops with the salt and pepper and set aside.

To prepare the Gorgonzola Sauce, cook the butter and garlic in a small sauté pan set on medium-high heat for 1-2 minutes, until the garlic and butter begin to brown. Add the chicken stock, cream, Gorgonzola and pepper. Boil the sauce for 10 minutes, until reduced and thickened. Stir in the chopped parsley.

While the sauce is reducing, grill the pork chops. Rub the chops and the grill with the olive oil. Place the grill rack 4-6 inches (10-15 cm) above medium-hot coals. Grill the chops for 3 minutes on each side, until the juices run clear when a small cut is made in the center. Transfer the chops to a serving platter and serve with the sauce on the side.

If you prefer not to grill the chops, they can be broiled or pan sautéed. Broil the chops for 4-5 minutes on each side 4-6 inches (10-15 cm) from the heat source. For sautéing, cover and cook the chops for 4-5 minutes on each side.

Wine Suggestion - Riesling

Pork Chops with Mustard Sauce

This very simple method of cooking pork chops is fragrant with herbs and the piquant flavor of mustard. The sweet pickle relish may sound unusual, but you have the Stellino word that it tastes great. The mustard actually gives the sauce a very nice bite.

Sprinkle both sides of the pork chops with the salt, pepper and flour, patting off the excess. Heat 2 tablespoons of the olive oil in a large sauté pan set on medium-high heat until sizzling, about 2 minutes. Cook the pork chops for 3-4 minutes on each side, until browned. Transfer to a plate and set aside.

Add the remaining olive oil to the same pan set on medium-high heat. Add the garlic, onion, thyme and rosemary and cook until the garlic begins to brown and the onion becomes translucent, about 3-4 minutes. Add the wine and boil until it's reduced by half, about 1-2 minutes. Stir in the chicken stock and bring to a boil. Add the mustard, parsley and pickle relish, if you wish. Return the pork chops and any accumulated juices to the pan and cook for 2 minutes to warm the chops and thicken the sauce. Transfer the chops to serving plates and top with the sauce.

Wine Suggestion - Semillon

4 pork chops, 1½ inches (4 cm) thick

¼ teaspoon salt

¼ teaspoon black pepper

2 tablespoons flour

3 tablespoons olive oil

4 garlic cloves, thickly sliced

½ onion, chopped

1 tablespoon chopped fresh thyme

1 tablespoon chopped fresh rosemary

¼ cup white wine

½ cup Chicken Stock (see page 225)

2 tablespoons Dijon mustard

1 tablespoon chopped fresh Italian parsley

2 tablespoons sweet pickle relish (optional)

Pork Chops with Prune-Port Sauce

SERVES 4

This recipe combines pork, a Sicilian favorite, with Madeira and prunes to create a dish that is full of the flavors of the Mediterranean. Cooking the pork chops at a high temperature for a short period of time ensures they will be moist and tender.

1½ tablespoons flour

3 teaspoons cumin

½ teaspoon salt

½ teaspoon black pepper

4 (1½ inch) (4 cm) thick
    pork chops, bone-in
    or boneless

2 tablespoons olive oil

1 tablespoon butter

½ cup chopped onion

4 garlic cloves, thickly sliced

2 tablespoons chopped fresh
    thyme or 2 teaspoons dried

¾ cup pitted, halved prunes
    (use canned prunes),
    juices drained and ¼ cup
    reserved)

¼ cup dry Madeira
    or Port wine

¾ cup Beef Stock
    (see page 226)

2 tablespoons chopped fresh
    Italian parsley

Combine the flour, 1½ teaspoons of the cumin, ¼ teaspoon of the salt and ¼ teaspoon of the pepper on a plate. Coat both sides of the pork chops with the seasoned flour, shaking off the excess. Set aside.

Heat 1 tablespoon of the olive oil and the butter in a large sauté pan set on medium-high heat until sizzling, about 1-2 minutes. Cook the pork chops for 3-4 minutes on each side, transfer to a plate and cover to keep warm. Set aside.

Add the remaining olive oil to the same pan set on medium-high heat. Cook the onion, garlic, the remaining cumin and the thyme for 3-4 minutes, until the garlic begins to brown. Add the prune halves and cook for 1 minute to heat through. Pour in the wine and boil until reduced by half, about 1 minute. Stir in the reserved prune juice, the beef stock, and the remaining salt and pepper. Boil the sauce for 3-4 minutes, until it begins to thicken and become syrupy. Stir in the parsley and return the pork chops and any accumulated juices to the pan. Cook for 2 minutes longer to warm the chops and further thicken the sauce. Transfer the chops to serving plates and drizzle with the sauce. Serve immediately.

Wine Suggestion - Cabernet Sauvignon

Steak with Red Wine Sauce

⌄

SERVES 2

Here is an elegant, but easy, dinner whose secret ingredient is definitely the beef marrow. Ask your butcher to cut the marrow from the middle of the bone, not near the joint.

Run a knife around the inside of the marrow bones to loosen the marrow, then push one end of the loosened marrow to remove it from the bone. Dice the marrow into ½-inch (1.5-cm) pieces and set aside. Discard the bones.

Sprinkle the steaks with ¼ teaspoon of the salt and ⅛ teaspoon of the pepper. Heat the vegetable oil in a medium sauté pan set on high heat until sizzling, about 2 minutes. Add the steaks, reduce the heat to medium-high and cook for 3 minutes per side for medium-rare. Transfer the steaks to serving plates and lightly cover with foil to keep warm while you prepare the sauce.

Discard the oil from the sauté pan and return it to medium-high heat. Add the butter, garlic, shallots or onion and parsley and cook until the shallots become translucent, about 1 minute. Stir in the wine and boil until reduced by half, about 2 minutes. Add the beef stock, the diced beef marrow and the remaining salt and pepper and boil until reduced by half, about 1 minute. To thicken the sauce, remove the pan from the heat and stir in the butter-flour paste. Return the pan to the heat and stir until thickened, about 1 minute. Stir in the cooked beef marrow. Top the steaks with the sauce and serve.

1½ pounds (700 g) beef marrow bones, cut 1-2 inches (2.5-5 cm) thick

2 (6-ounce) (175-g) beef tenderloin steaks, 1½ inches (4 cm) thick

½ teaspoon salt

¼ teaspoon black pepper

1 tablespoon vegetable oil

1 tablespoon butter

2 garlic cloves, thickly sliced

3 tablespoons finely chopped shallots or white onion

2 tablespoons chopped fresh Italian parsley

½ cup dry red wine

¼ cup Beef Stock (see page 226)

1 teaspoon soft butter mixed with 1 teaspoon flour

Cook's Tip

To prepare this recipe for four people, just double all the ingredients. The sauce will take twice as long to reduce because of the larger volume of liquid.

Wine Suggestion - Merlot

French Pepper Steaks

A zesty, pepper-crusted steak with a lovely, subtle shallot-brandy sauce. Have all your ingredients and side dishes ready, because the whole dinner can be prepared in about 15 minutes.

1½ tablespoons whole black peppercorns

2 (8-ounce) (225-g) New York steaks, 1½-2 inches (4-5 cm) thick

½ teaspoon salt

2 tablespoons vegetable oil

1 tablespoon butter

2 garlic cloves, thickly sliced

3 tablespoons finely chopped shallots or white onion

2 tablespoons chopped fresh Italian parsley

¼ cup brandy

½ cup Beef Stock (see page 226)

1 teaspoon soft butter mixed with 1 teaspoon flour

Place the peppercorns on a cutting board and crush them with the bottom of a heavy pan (place the pan over the peppercorns and press down). Sprinkle the steaks with ¼ teaspoon of the salt and then press each side in the crushed peppercorns so they are evenly coated.

Heat the vegetable oil in a large sauté pan set on high heat until sizzling, about 2 minutes. Place the steaks in the pan and reduce the heat to medium-high. Cook 1½-inch (4-cm) steaks for 3-4 minutes per side for medium-rare, and 2-inch (5-cm) steaks for 5-6 minutes per side for medium-rare. Remove the steaks to a plate and set aside. Discard the oil from the pan.

Add the butter, garlic, shallots or onion and parsley to the same pan set on medium-high heat and cook, stirring, until the shallots or onion become translucent, about 1 minute. Stir in the brandy and boil until reduced by half, about 1 minute. Add the beef stock and the remaining salt, bring to a boil and cook until reduced by half, about 2 minutes. Remove the pan from the heat and stir in the butter-flour paste. Return the pan to the heat and stir until thickened, about 1 minute. Transfer the steaks to serving plates, top with the sauce and serve.

Cook's Tip

If you would like to prepare this dish for four people, simply double all the ingredients and cook the steaks and the sauce in two pans.

Wine Suggestion - Pinot Noir

Italian Meat Pockets

The savory salami-cheese filling in a pocket of tender beef has a very Sicilian heritage, but also a universal appeal. Simple, but unique, this dish is sure to spark interest in even your most jaded dinner companions.

Place 1 slice of the salami and 1 slice of the cheese on half of a beef slice. Fold the meat slice in half over the filling and secure the end with a toothpick. Repeat with the remaining beef slices. Chop the remaining salami slices and set aside. Mix the salt, pepper and flour on a plate and coat both sides of the meat rolls with the mixture, patting off any excess.

Heat 2 tablespoons of the olive oil and the butter in a large sauté pan set on high heat until smoking, about 2-3 minutes. Add the meat pockets and cook for 30 seconds on each side - you will need to do this in batches. Transfer the browned meat to a plate and add the remaining oil to the same pan. Add the onion, garlic, red pepper flakes, the reserved chopped salami and the oregano and cook for 1 minute, until the onion and garlic begin to brown. Stir in the Marsala and boil until reduced by half, about 1 minute. Add the tomato sauce, beef stock, bay leaf and parsley and cook for 1-2 minutes, until reduced and slightly thickened. Return the browned meat to the pan and heat for 1-2 minutes. Serve immediately.

Cook's Tip

If you can't find beef scallopine, purchase 1 pound (450 g) of beef eye of round or top sirloin. Remove any fat or gristle, then cut slices ½ inch (1.5 cm) thick, cutting across the grain. Place each slice of meat between 2 sheets of plastic wrap and pound, down and out from the center, until ¼ inch (6 mm) thick and approximately 3 x 6 inches (8 x 15 cm) in size.

Wine Suggestion - Syrah

24 thin slices salami
   (about 4 ounces [115 g]),
   preferably soppressata
   or Napoli

8 slices provolone cheese
   (4 ounces [115 g]),
   cut in half

1 pound (450 g) beef for
   scallopine, pounded thin
   (you should have at least
   16 pieces, see Cook's Tip)

¼ teaspoon salt

¼ teaspoon black pepper

2½ tablespoons flour

3 tablespoons olive oil

1 tablespoon butter

¼ cup chopped onion

4 garlic cloves, thickly sliced

¼ teaspoon red pepper flakes

¼ teaspoon oregano

¼ cup dry Marsala wine

½ cup Tomato Sauce
   (see page 222)

½ cup Beef Stock
   (see page 226)

1 bay leaf

2 tablespoons chopped fresh
   Italian parsley

Beef and Bell Pepper Stew

The beef in this colorful stew cooks until it becomes fork-tender, while the peppers provide a mysterious subtle sweetness. (Illustrated in this section.)

1½ pounds (700 g) cubed
  beef stew meat

¾ teaspoon salt

½ teaspoon black pepper

1½ tablespoons flour

4 tablespoons olive oil

4 garlic cloves, thickly sliced

¼ teaspoon red pepper flakes

3 large bell peppers, preferably
  1 each red, yellow and
  green, cut into 1½-inch
  (4-cm) pieces

1 onion, cut into 1½-inch
  (4-cm) pieces

2 teaspoons thyme

2 bay leaves

1 cup dry red wine

3 cups Beef Stock
  (see page 226)

2 cups Tomato Sauce
  (see page 222)

2 tablespoons chopped fresh
  Italian parsley

Sprinkle the meat cubes with the salt, pepper and flour, shaking off any excess. Heat 3 tablespoons of the olive oil in a Dutch oven set on high heat until sizzling, about 2 minutes. Add the meat in a single layer, being careful not to crowd the meat pieces - cook in 2 batches, if necessary. Cook the meat until well-browned on all sides, about 3-4 minutes. Transfer the meat to a plate or bowl with a slotted spoon. Set aside.

Add the remaining oil to the same pan set on high heat. Add the garlic, red pepper flakes, bell peppers, onion, thyme and bay leaves. Cook until the peppers are beginning to soften and the onion is translucent, about 4-5 minutes. Return the browned meat to the pan along with any juices that have accumulated. Stir in the wine and boil until reduced by half, about 4 minutes. Add the beef stock and tomato sauce and bring to a boil. Reduce the heat to low and simmer, with the lid slightly ajar, for 1 hour. Remove the lid and cook 30 minutes longer. Stir in the parsley and the stew is ready to serve.

Cook's Tip

To add a sweet-and-sour dimension to the stew, boil 1 tablespoon sugar and 2 tablespoons balsamic vinegar in a small saucepan set on high heat until reduced by half and quite syrupy, about 2 minutes. Stir the syrup and 1 teaspoon cocoa powder into the finished stew and cook for 2 minutes.

Wine Suggestion - Merlot

Braised Beef and Olives

The flavor sensation provided by the simple addition of bacon and olives makes a surprising difference to familiar beef stew. The powerful aroma from the herbs and wine is also heightened by the contrast of bright orange zest.

Sprinkle the stew meat with the salt and pepper and coat evenly with 1½ tablespoons of the flour, shaking off any excess. Heat 3 tablespoons of the olive oil in a Dutch oven set on high heat until sizzling, about 2 minutes. Add the meat in 2 batches and cook until well browned, about 3-4 minutes. Transfer the meat to a bowl with a slotted spoon and set aside.

Add the remaining oil to the pan set on high heat. Add the garlic, onion, thyme, rosemary, sage, bay leaves, bacon and mushrooms. Cook until the onion is translucent and the mushrooms are beginning to soften, about 4-5 minutes. Stir in the remaining flour and cook for 1-2 minutes. Return the meat and any accumulated juices to the pan. Stir in the wine and boil until reduced by half, about 4 minutes. It will be necessary to stir a bit while the wine is reducing because the flour will thicken the sauce. Add the beef stock and olives and bring to a boil. Reduce the heat to low and simmer, with the lid slightly ajar, for 1 hour. Remove the lid and cook for 30 minutes. Add the orange zest to the stew during the last 5 minutes of cooking. Stir in the parsley and the stew is ready to be served with the parsley potatoes on the side.

Wine Suggestion - Cabernet Franc

1½ pounds (700 g) beef stew meat, cubed

¼ teaspoon salt

¼ teaspoon black pepper

3½ tablespoons flour

4 tablespoons olive oil

10 garlic cloves, halved

1 onion, chopped

2 teaspoons thyme

2 teaspoons rosemary

2 teaspoons sage

2 bay leaves

2 slices thick bacon, diced

¾ pound (350 g) mushrooms, quartered

1 cup dry red wine

5 cups Beef Stock (see page 226)

1 cup pitted green olives, quartered

1½ teaspoons grated orange zest

2 tablespoons chopped fresh Italian parsley

1 recipe Parsley New Potatoes (see page 160)

Mediterranean Shepherd's Pie

Shepherd's Pie has been enjoyed with gusto by Englishmen for centuries - now it's the Mediterranean's turn! In this version, a hearty stew is topped with oven-browned mashed potatoes that are flavored with Romano cheese.

1 recipe Romano Mashed
   Potatoes (see page 164)

½ pound (225 g) beef stew
   meat, cubed

½ pound (225 g) boneless
   chicken thighs, cut into
   1-inch (2.5-cm) pieces

½ pound (225 g) Italian
   sausage, cut into ¼-inch
   (6-mm) slices

½ teaspoon salt

½ teaspoon black pepper

2½ tablespoons flour

3 tablespoons olive oil

4 garlic cloves, thickly sliced

1 onion, chopped

2 carrots, cut into ½-inch
   (1.5-cm) pieces

2 celery stalks, cut into ½-inch
   (1.5-cm) pieces

1 teaspoon paprika

2 teaspoons thyme

(continued)

Prepare the Romano Mashed Potatoes and keep warm until needed. The mashed potatoes can be prepared ahead and refrigerated until you're ready to assemble the pie. Warm the potatoes in the microwave before trying to spread them over the pie.

Place the stew meat, chicken and sausage on a large plate and sprinkle with the salt, pepper and 1½ tablespoons of the flour, tossing to coat the meat evenly. Shake off any excess flour. Heat the olive oil in a Dutch oven set on high heat until sizzling, about 2 minutes. Add the beef cubes and cook until well browned on all sides, about 3-4 minutes. Transfer to a bowl with a slotted spoon and set aside. Repeat with the chicken and sausage.

To the same pan set on medium-high heat, add the garlic, onion, carrots, celery, paprika, thyme, oregano, sage, bay leaves, cinnamon and nutmeg. Cook until the onion is translucent, about 4-5 minutes. Stir in the remaining flour, the tomato paste and sugar and cook for 1-2 minutes. Return the meats and any accumulated juices to the pan. Stir in the Marsala and boil until reduced by half, about 4 minutes. It will be necessary to stir a bit while the wine is reducing because the flour will thicken the sauce. Add the beef stock and bring to a boil. Reduce the heat to medium and simmer for 30 minutes, uncovered. Add the peas to the stew during the last 5 minutes of cooking.

Preheat the oven to 400° F (200° C). Pour the stew into a 9 x 13-inch (23 x 33-cm) baking dish. Drop the mashed potatoes by spoonfuls on the stew and gently smooth them out with the bottom of the spoon or a knife. Don't press too hard or you'll push them down into the stew. Brush the top with the melted butter and sprinkle with the Romano cheese. Bake for 30 minutes, until the potatoes are browned and the stew is bubbling. Remove from the oven and let cool for 10 minutes before serving.

Cook's Tip

You can make an attractive design in the potatoes by lightly running the tines of a fork across the top after they've been brushed with the butter.

Wine Suggestion - Syrah

1 teaspoon oregano

2 teaspoons sage

2 bay leaves

½ teaspoon cinnamon

½ teaspoon nutmeg

2 tablespoons tomato paste

1 teaspoon sugar

1 cup dry Marsala wine

2½ cups Beef Stock
   (see page 226)

1½ cups frozen peas, thawed

2 tablespoons melted butter

¼ cup grated Pecorino
   Romano cheese

Rack of Lamb with Mustard, Garlic and Rosemary

SERVES 4 TO 6

When your guests see a rack of lamb coming to the table, they know it's a special evening, but they won't know how special until they actually taste the rosemary-garlic-mustard-encrusted slices on their plate. You can prepare the crust a day ahead of time. Keep it covered, in the refrigerator, and take it out about 30 minutes before roasting.

4 tablespoons chopped garlic

4 tablespoons chopped
   fresh rosemary

1½ teaspoons salt

1½ teaspoons black pepper

2 (2-pound) (900-g) racks
   of lamb

4 tablespoons Dijon mustard

¾ cup Italian Bread Crumbs
   (see page 230)

½ pound (225 g) carrots,
   cut into large chunks

½ pound (225 g) new
   potatoes, cut into eighths

2 heads of garlic, separated
   into unpeeled cloves

¼ pound (115 g) unpeeled
   small shallots, cut in half

4 tablespoons olive oil

3 tablespoons tomato paste

½ pound (225 g) green beans,
   ends trimmed, cut in half

¼ cup dry Madeira
   or red wine

1 cup Beef Stock
   (see page 226)

2 teaspoons cornstarch mixed
   with 2 teaspoons beef stock
   (slurry)

Combine the garlic, rosemary, 1 teaspoon of the salt and 1¼ teaspoons of the pepper and chop to a paste-like consistency. Poke a few holes in the meaty part of the lamb racks with a toothpick or skewer. Brush both sides of the racks with 2 tablespoons of the mustard and coat with the rosemary/garlic mixture. Pat the bread crumbs over both sides to form a uniform coat. Set aside.

Cook the carrots and potatoes in a pot of boiling water for 5 minutes. Drain well and place in a large bowl with the garlic cloves, shallots, 3 tablespoons of the olive oil, the tomato paste and the remaining salt and pepper. Mix until the vegetables are evenly coated.

Preheat the oven to 450° F (230° C). Place the lamb racks on a roasting rack. Set the rack on a large baking sheet with sides or a large roasting pan that has been brushed with the remaining olive oil. Place the vegetable mixture around the roasting rack on the baking sheet. (Place the green beans in the bowl and toss them around to pick up any leftover oil and tomato paste remaining in the bowl and set aside.) Roast in the preheated oven for 30-40 minutes, until the internal temperature reaches 130° F (54° C) for medium-rare meat. After the first 15 minutes of cooking, turn the racks over and distribute the green beans over the carrots and potatoes.

When the lamb has reached the desired doneness, remove from the oven and let rest on a cutting board for 5-10 minutes, lightly covered with aluminum foil. Transfer the vegetables to a bowl and cover to keep warm. Pour the Madeira or red wine into the baking sheet, stirring to scrape up any brown bits from the bottom, then transfer into a small saucepan and boil until reduced by half over medium-high heat, about 1-2 minutes. Stir in the remaining mustard and the beef stock and simmer over low heat for 5 minutes. Remove from the heat and stir in the cornstarch slurry. Return to the heat and boil for 1 minute to thicken.

Slice the lamb into individual chops and serve with the roasted vegetables and the sauce.

Wine Suggestion - Cabernet Sauvignon

Just like the first time I cooked it for my parents, I am still fascinated by the ease of preparation and the wonderful flavor of this hearty dish.

Turkish Kebabs

⌄

SERVES 4 TO 6

Skewers of meat and vegetables are sold everywhere in the Eastern Mediterranean, both in fancy restaurants and by casual vendors standing on street corners. Marinating the meat in the spicy yogurt gives it a bold flavor and a golden hue that contrasts beautifully with the bright red tomatoes. (Illustrated in this section.)

YOGURT MARINADE

1 (32-ounce) (900-g)
    container low-fat or
    nonfat plain yogurt

3 garlic cloves, finely chopped

¼ cup lemon juice

1 teaspoon salt

½ teaspoon black pepper

1½ teaspoons cumin

1 teaspoon saffron powder
    or turmeric

¾ teaspoon cinnamon

¼ teaspoon cayenne

4 tablespoons chopped
    fresh Italian parsley

4 tablespoons chopped
    fresh mint

(continued)

The day before serving, combine all the Yogurt Marinade ingredients in a large bowl and mix well. If you prefer using a food processor, place all the marinade ingredients except the parsley and mint in the processor bowl (the garlic doesn't need to be chopped beforehand) and process to a smooth consistency. Stir the herbs in by hand. Set aside.

To assemble the Kebabs, skewer the ingredients on 9 long bamboo or metal skewers in the following order: onion, meat, tomato, mushroom. Repeat this 2 more times so that you have 3 pieces of each ingredient each skewer. If you have extra pieces, just put them on at the end; some of the kebabs will have 4 pieces of meat instead of 3.

Place the kebabs on a large baking sheet and pour three-fourths of the yogurt marinade over them. Roll the kebabs in the marinade to coat them completely, cover with plastic wrap and refrigerate overnight. Reserve the remaining marinade separately in the refrigerator.

The day of serving, you can grill or broil the marinated kebabs. If using a gas grill, preheat the grill to medium temperature, or for charcoal grilling heat the coals until white hot, then let them cool to medium hot (you should be able to hold your hand over the coals for 3 seconds) and place the grill 4-6 inches (10-15 cm) above the coals. Brush the grill rack with olive oil to keep the kebabs from sticking. Cook the kebabs for 10 minutes for medium-well doneness, turning several times, lightly brushing them with some of the oil.

To broil the kebabs, place them on an oiled baking sheet and lightly brush with some of the oil. Broil 4-6 inches (10-15 cm) from the heat source for 5 minutes on each side or until the meat is the desired doneness.

Serve the kebabs over the rice pilaf with the reserved marinade/sauce for dipping. (Don't use any leftover marinade that the kebabs were marinated in as a sauce; it should be discarded.)

Wine Suggestion - Chardonnay

KEBABS

2 onions, cut into eighths (size should be about the same as the pieces of meat)

1½ pounds (700 g) boneless leg of lamb, fat trimmed, cut into 1- to 1½-inch (2.5- to 4-cm) pieces
or
1½ pounds (700 g) skinless boneless chicken breasts, cut into 1- to 1½-inch (2.5- to 4-cm) pieces
or
1½ pounds (700 g) boneless beef sirloin steak, cut into 1- to 1½-inch (2.5- to 4-cm) pieces

9 Roma tomatoes, quartered

36 small button mushrooms, stems cut off

¼ cup olive oil

1 recipe Rice Pilaf with Currants and Pine Nuts (see page 170)

Moussaka

Moussaka is a Greek classic that has found a huge and appreciative audience around the world. Tucked under the layers of spiced lamb and tender eggplant you will discover thinly sliced potatoes, which give it a Turkish flair. Ask your butcher specifically for lean lamb, ground without any fatty trimmings. Beef is the perfect substitute if you can't find lamb.

2 (1½-pound) (700-g) eggplants

2¼ teaspoons salt

6 tablespoons olive oil

1½ pounds (700 g) potatoes, peeled, cut into ⅛-inch (3-mm) slices and patted dry

¾ teaspoon black pepper

1½ pounds (700 g) ground lamb or beef

1 onion, thinly sliced

4 garlic cloves, thickly sliced

2 bay leaves

¾ teaspoon cinnamon

½ teaspoon allspice

¼ teaspoon nutmeg

2 teaspoons thyme

½ cup red wine

1¼ cups Tomato Sauce (see page 222)

1 cup Beef Stock (see page 226)

2 cups Béchamel Sauce (see page 228)

½ cup freshly grated Parmigiano Reggiano cheese

Cut the eggplants crosswise into ½-inch (1.5-cm) thick slices. Sprinkle with 1½ teaspoons of the salt and stack in a colander. Place a plate on top, weight it down and drain for 20 minutes. Pat the slices dry with paper towels and set aside.

Preheat the oven to 425° F (220° C). Brush a nonstick baking sheet and both sides of the eggplant slices with 3 tablespoons of the olive oil. Place the slices in a single layer on the baking sheet and cook for 25 minutes, until lightly browned. Set aside.

Heat 2 tablespoons of the remaining olive oil in a large sauté pan set on high heat until sizzling, about 2 minutes. Add the potatoes, sprinkle with ¼ teaspoon of the salt and ¼ teaspoon of the pepper and cook until they begin to brown, about 5 minutes. Transfer the potatoes to a 9 x 13-inch (23 x 33-cm) baking dish, spreading them evenly. Set aside.

Heat the remaining olive oil in the same pan set on high heat. Add the ground lamb or beef and cook for 6-7 minutes, until browned. Using a slotted spoon, transfer the browned meat to a bowl and drain all but 2 tablespoons of fat from the pan. Return the pan to high heat and cook the onion, garlic, bay leaves, cinnamon, allspice, nutmeg, thyme and the remaining salt and pepper and cook for 3 minutes. Return the browned meat to the pan and cook for 1 minute. Stir in the wine and cook until reduced by half, about 1-2 minutes. Add the tomato sauce and beef stock and bring to a boil. Reduce the heat to medium and simmer for 10 minutes, until the sauce has thickened.

Preheat the oven to 375° F (190° C). To assemble the dish, arrange half the reserved eggplant slices over the potatoes in the baking dish. Top with the meat sauce and then with the remaining eggplant slices. Pour the béchamel sauce over the top and sprinkle with the grated Parmigiano Reggiano cheese. Bake for 45 minutes, until the top is golden brown. Remove from the oven and cool for 10-15 minutes. Cut into 8 squares and serve.

Cook's Tip

This is a great dish to assemble and bake a day ahead. The flavors will be better the next day and it will cut more easily. Individual pieces can be reheated in the microwave or the whole dish can be reheated, uncovered, in a 350° F (180° C) oven for 1 hour.

Wine Suggestion - Gewürztraminer

The unforgettable flavors of this traditional dish will carry your imagination along the white sand beaches of the Greek islands.

Ginger Tuna

Snowy white tuna steaks with crisp brown edges are served with a remarkably simple butter-lemon-ginger sauce. You'll be surprised how quickly it cooks - just ten minutes! Make sure you don't overcook, because when the tuna is set aside and covered with the foil, it will continue cooking. I assure you that when it's time to serve, the tuna will be perfectly done.

4 (6- to 8-ounce) (175- to 225-g) yellowfin tuna steaks, cut 1 inch (2.5 cm) thick

½ teaspoon salt

¼ teaspoon black pepper

3 tablespoons olive oil

4 tablespoons butter

4 garlic cloves, chopped

1 tablespoon grated fresh gingerroot

⅛ teaspoon red pepper flakes

2 teaspoons grated lemon zest

3 tablespoons chopped shallots or white onion

½ cup white wine

2 tablespoons chopped fresh Italian parsley

Sprinkle the tuna steaks with ¼ teaspoon of the salt and the pepper. Heat the olive oil in a large sauté pan set on medium-high heat until sizzling, about 2 minutes. Add the tuna steaks and cook for 2 minutes per side. The steaks will be well-browned on the outside but still raw inside. Transfer to a plate and cover with foil. Set aside.

Melt 1 tablespoon of the butter in the same pan set on high heat. Add the garlic, ginger, red pepper flakes, lemon zest and shallots or onion. Cook for 1 minute. Stir in the wine, scraping up any brown bits from the bottom of the pan. Add the parsley and the remaining salt and cook until reduced by half, about 2 minutes. Remove the pan from the heat and stir in the remaining butter until it's completely melted. Place the tuna on serving plates and top with the sauce.

Cook's Tip

Shallots, a petite member of the onion family, resemble both onions and garlic. Wrapped in a reddish-brown to yellow-brown papery skin like an onion, shallots are divided into small segmented cloves like garlic with a delicate flavor and tender texture. For this reason they are ideal for cooked sauces such as this recipe.

Wine Suggestion - Pinot Noir

Whole Fish Baked in a Salt Crust

⌄

SERVES 4

This classic Mediterranean cooking method provides a hard crust that preserves all the juices and flavors from the herbs, lemon and fish during baking. It's also very simple to put together. Bring it whole to the table and I guarantee an impressive, memorable meal.

Preheat the oven to 350° F (180° C). Spread 2 cups of the rock salt in the bottom of 2 (9 x 13-inch) (23 x 33-cm) baking dishes. Sprinkle each dish with ½ cup of the water. Place one of the fish in each dish at an angle - it's okay if the tail is sticking out a little. Sprinkle the inside of each fish with the table salt and the pepper. Stuff each fish with 4 of the lemon slices, 4 sprigs of parsley, 4 sprigs of thyme, 4 basil leaves and 2 sliced garlic cloves. Top each fish with 4-5 cups of the remaining rock salt, covering so that no skin is showing, other than the tail. The layer of salt will be about ½ inch (1.5 cm) thick. Sprinkle with the remaining ½ cup of the water.

Place the baking dishes side-by-side in the oven and bake for 40-45 minutes. Remove from the oven and chip the crust away with a wooden spoon to expose the fish. Lift the fish out of the dish with a large spatula and brush away any remaining salt. Place both fish on a large platter, bring to the table and serve with the red pepper sauce or aioli on the side.

Cook's Tip

If you bring the dish whole to the table, have a cutting board and an extra plate for scraps and bones. Of course, if you don't want to fuss with filleting the fish at the table, do it in the kitchen.

Wine Suggestion - Cabernet Sauvignon

12-14 cups rock salt

2 cups water

2 (2-pound) (900-g) whole striped sea bass, scaled and gutted, heads and tails left on

¾ teaspoon table salt

½ teaspoon black pepper

8 thin lemon slices

8 sprigs fresh Italian parsley

8 sprigs fresh thyme

8 large fresh basil leaves

4 garlic cloves, thickly sliced

1 recipe Provençal Red Pepper Sauce (see page 221)
or
1 recipe Aioli (see page 220)

Baked Fish Fillets

⌄

SERVES 4

Start this easy and impressive fish dish on the stove and finish baking in the oven with the thick tomato-eggplant sauce. The optional sweet-and-sour finish comes from a balsamic vinegar syrup stirred in at the very end, which truly adds a whole new dimension to the dish.

1 pound (450 g) eggplant, cut into medium cubes

1 teaspoon salt

4 (6- to 8-ounce) (175- to 225-g) Chilean sea bass fillets, or any thick firm-fleshed white saltwater fish

½ teaspoon black pepper

5 tablespoons olive oil

4 garlic cloves, thickly sliced

¼ teaspoon red pepper flakes

1 (28-ounce) (790-g) can peeled Italian tomatoes, drained, chopped and juices reserved separately

8 whole basil leaves

¼ teaspoon oregano

2 tablespoons balsamic vinegar (optional)

1 tablespoon sugar (optional)

Sprinkle the eggplant cubes with ¼ teaspoon of the salt and put in a colander. Place a dish over the eggplant and weight it down. Drain for 20 minutes and pat dry with a towel. Set aside.

Sprinkle the fish fillets with ¼ teaspoon of the salt and ¼ teaspoon of the pepper. Heat 1 tablespoon of the olive oil in a large sauté pan set on medium-high heat until sizzling, about 2 minutes. Put the fish fillets in the pan and reduce the heat to medium. Cook for 2 minutes on each side, until well browned. Transfer the fillets to a plate and set aside.

In the same pan, heat 3 tablespoons of the remaining olive oil over high heat until sizzling, about 2 minutes. Cook the eggplant in the hot oil until well browned, about 5 minutes. Transfer the eggplant to a 9 x 13-inch (23 x 33-cm) baking dish and set aside.

Preheat the oven to 400° F (200° C). Add the remaining olive oil, garlic and red pepper flakes to the same pan set on high heat and cook until sizzling, about 2 minutes. Add the drained tomatoes, basil, oregano, the remaining ½ teaspoon of salt and the remaining ¼ teaspoon of black pepper. Cook for 2 minutes. Add half of the reserved tomato juices, discarding the remaining juices. Bring to a boil and cook until reduced by half and thickened, about 4-5 minutes. Pour the sauce over the eggplant and top with the fish fillets, pushing the fillets lightly into the sauce. Bake, uncovered, for 15-20 minutes. Transfer the fish and sauce to a serving dish. If you wish to try the sweet-and-sour finish, combine the optional balsamic vinegar and sugar in a small saucepan set on high heat and boil until reduced by half, about 2 minutes. Drizzle over the fish before serving.

Wine Suggestion - Merlot

North African Mussels and Clams

Make this spicy, fragrant shellfish dish the center of a fun evening. Just carry it to the table with a bowl for everyone to throw their shells and let the good times roll. I think the best part could be the tomato-infused liquid into which you can dip your crusty bread - don't miss a drop!

Place the clams and mussels in a large pan or bowl of salted water (⅓ cup salt to 4 quarts [3.75 l] water). Let the shellfish sit for 1 hour to disgorge any sand, then scrub with a small stiff brush to remove any sand or algae from the shells. Discard any with broken shells. Use a small knife to scrape or cut the beard (the small hairy tuft protruding from one side of the shell) from the mussels. Rinse all the shellfish well.

Heat the olive oil in a large sauté pan set on high heat until almost smoking, about 3 minutes. Add the cleaned mussels, clams, garlic, green onions, parsley, cumin, curry powder, saffron or turmeric, red pepper flakes and salt. Stir well and cook for 2 minutes. Add the wine, stirring up any brown bits from the bottom. Stir in the clam juice and tomato sauce, cover and cook for 3-5 minutes, until the mussels and clams have all opened. Discard any that don't open. Remove the mussels and clams to a large serving bowl and cover to keep warm. Cook the sauce over high heat to reduce it slightly, about 3 minutes. Pour over the shellfish and serve with slices of pita bread to dip in the sauce.

Wine Suggestion - Gewürztraminer

1 pound (450 g) clams
  (preferably Manila),
  rinsed

1 pound (450 g) mussels,
  rinsed

2 tablespoons olive oil

4 garlic cloves, thickly sliced

1 bunch green onions,
  including 2 inches (5 cm)
  green parts, thinly sliced

2 tablespoons chopped fresh
  Italian parsley

½ teaspoon cumin

½ teaspoon curry powder

¼ teaspoon saffron powder
  or turmeric

¼ teaspoon red pepper flakes

½ teaspoon salt

½ cup white wine

¼ cup clam juice

1 cup Tomato Sauce
  (see page 222)

SIDE DISHES

Ferruccio and Carlito

*A*s a boy growing up in Sicily, I first became acquainted with many of the epicurean wonders of the Mediterranean region through a local character known as *Ferruccio le Recounter,* "the Storyteller."

Ferruccio was an old friend of my father, as fine a raconteur as he was a dinner guest. In fact, he was one of the blessed few who had complete autonomy in my mother's kitchen - a right he had earned over the years as he introduced an array of exotic dishes he had discovered during his travels abroad. He would cook for us some of these wonderful recipes, accompanying each one with a story of where he discovered it and under what circumstances. A meal with Ferruccio was like being a spectator at a dinner theater.

I vividly recall one summer evening, when we were dining al fresco on my parents' veranda, and Ferruccio was "performing." The story that accompanied this meal took place during one of his car trips to Spain some years before. He had found himself stranded in a mountain village when his car, a Fiat "Cinquecento" - popularly known as the sardine can on wheels - broke down, a not uncommon occurrence on that trip.

As he wandered the streets waiting for the car to be repaired, he was caught in a sudden and violent rain storm, with no umbrella and no place to shelter. Yet, Ferruccio, a man of unequaled optimism, kept on walking, as mindless as any tourist enjoying the sights of the deserted village.

Suddenly he was confronted by a large shaggy dog, dripping wet, standing in the middle of the alley in front of him. Fearful at first, Ferruccio proceeded with caution. Suddenly the dog leaped forward and Ferruccio fell to the rain-soaked street, closing his eyes as he crossed his arms to cover his face. Unexpectedly he felt the warmth of the dog's breath and the rough caress of his tongue licking him all over.

Even as Ferruccio wrestled to his feet, he heard a voice in the distance calling "Carlito! Carlito!" From around the corner came running an old man, holding a large black umbrella, clearly the owner of the overly friendly pooch. Before Ferruccio could say a word, the old man had helped him to his feet and, taking him firmly by the arm, guided him to a nearby doorway - his rescuer's home, as it turned out. There, in the dining room, a group of a dozen or more people were gathered around a large table. Upon seeing Ferruccio, dripping and disheveled, and hearing the old man's hasty explanation, they invited him to dry out and join their meal.

And quite a meal it turned out to be! A fragrant chicken with almond sauce dominated the table, surrounded by a supporting cast of dishes too numerous to take in at one glance. One of these dishes, which turned out to be among Ferruccio's favorites, Spinach with Raisins and Pine Nuts, is included in this section. My interpretation of the chicken dish, Spanish Chicken with Almond Sauce, is in the Entrées section.

The meal passed in noisy camaraderie as Ferruccio inevitably worked his charm in spite of some language barrier. While it may be impossible for me to recount Ferruccio's story with the same panache with which he entertained my family, many of the dishes that he re-created for us are presented here in the spirit of discovery and friendship that Ferruccio enjoyed on that rainy afternoon.

Offerings of food
have been breaking down barriers
for centuries.

ESTEE LAUDER (1908-)

Oven Roasted Vegetables

Roasting is a simple technique that brings out extra sweetness from vegetables. From pan to oven to table, it is an easy way to add vegetables to any meal.

½ pound (225 g) carrots,
   cut into 1-inch (2.5-cm)
   chunks

½ pound (225 g) new
   potatoes, cut into eighths

2 heads of garlic, separated
   into unpeeled cloves

¼ pound (115 g) unpeeled
   small shallots, cut in half

3 tablespoons olive oil

3 tablespoons tomato paste

½ teaspoon salt

¼ teaspoon black pepper

½ pound (225 g) green beans,
   ends trimmed, cut in half

Preheat the oven to 450° F (230° C). Cook the carrots and potatoes in a large pot of boiling water for 5 minutes. Drain well and place in a large bowl with the garlic cloves, shallots, olive oil, tomato paste, salt and pepper. Mix until the vegetables are evenly coated. Spread the vegetables in a medium baking dish or sheet and bake for 15 minutes. Add the green beans to the same bowl and toss them around to pick up any remaining oil and tomato paste in the bowl. Remove the vegetables from the oven and spread the green beans evenly on top. Bake for another 15-20 minutes, until the vegetables are tender. Serve immediately.

Provençal Baked Vegetables

My version of the French classic has it all: gorgeous colors, irresistible aroma and flavors. It works well warm, or at room temperature. Take it on your next picnic or serve at a buffet.

Preheat the oven to 400° F (200° C). Heat 2 tablespoons of the olive oil in a large sauté pan set on high heat until sizzling, about 2 minutes. Add the onions, garlic, rosemary, ½ teaspoon of the salt and ⅛ teaspoon of the pepper. Cook until the onions are translucent and beginning to brown. Spread over the bottom of a 9 x 13-inch (23 x 33-cm) baking dish.

Arrange the slices of zucchini and tomatoes in alternating rows over the onions. Overlap them as much as you need to in order to use all the vegetable slices. Mix the remaining olive oil with the mustard and brush the vegetables with the mixture, using all of it. Sprinkle with the remaining salt and pepper and bake until the vegetables are lightly browned and wrinkled, about 1 hour. Serve hot or warm.

4 tablespoons olive oil

1½ pounds (700 g) onions, peeled, cut in half lengthwise and thinly sliced

6 garlic cloves, thickly sliced

2 teaspoons chopped fresh rosemary

¾ teaspoon salt

¼ teaspoon black pepper

2 zucchini, cut into ¼-inch (6-mm) slices

1 pound (450 g) Roma tomatoes, cut into ¼-inch (6-mm) slices

1 tablespoon coarsely ground mustard

Broccoli with Roasted Peppers

Roasted red peppers from a jar make this extra easy - yet it still provides a powerful blend of seductive flavors.

5 tablespoons olive oil

1 pound (450 g) broccoli,
   cut into florets, stems
   peeled and cut into
   ½-inch (1.5-cm) dice

4 garlic cloves, thickly sliced

¾ cup roasted red peppers,
   roughly chopped

¼ cup white wine

¼ cup Chicken Stock
   (see page 225)

¼ teaspoon salt

⅛ teaspoon black pepper

Heat 4 tablespoons of the olive oil in a large sauté pan set on high heat until sizzling, about 2 minutes. Add the broccoli and cook for 3-4 minutes, until the edges begin to brown. Transfer to a bowl with a slotted spoon and set aside. Add the remaining oil to the same pan set on high heat. Add the garlic and red peppers and cook until the garlic begins to brown, about 1-2 minutes. Stir in the wine, chicken stock, salt and pepper. Return the broccoli to the pan, cover, and cook for 2 minutes. Remove the lid and give everything a good toss. Cook until the remaining liquid has almost completely evaporated, about 1 minute. The broccoli is ready to serve.

Cook's Tip

As a flavor enhancement, top the finished broccoli with ¼ cup of freshly grated Parmigiano Reggiano cheese or ½ cup of crumbled feta or goat cheese.

Cauliflower with Nutmeg

This dish's simple flavors are the perfect contrast for an especially rich entrée - perhaps a special occasion or a holiday meal?

Preheat the oven to 400° F (200° C). Place the cauliflower in an 8-inch (20-cm) square baking dish. Pour the milk over the cauliflower, sprinkle with the nutmeg, salt and pepper. Cover with foil and bake for 35 minutes. Remove the cauliflower with a slotted spoon and serve with some of the hot milk spooned on top.

1 pound (450 g)
    cauliflower florets

1½ cups milk

¼ teaspoon nutmeg

½ teaspoon salt

⅛ teaspoon black pepper

Cook's Tip

The leftover milk can be strained and saved for several days in the refrigerator for use in making Béchamel Sauce (page 228). You won't need to add nutmeg to the sauce recipe.

Ginger-Glazed Carrots

SERVES 4 TO 6

The glaze from the ginger, butter and sugar makes this very sweet - almost like candy. (Illustrated in the Entrées section.)

2 tablespoons butter

2 tablespoons sugar

1 tablespoon fresh chopped
   or grated gingerroot

1½ pounds (700 g) carrots,
   peeled and cut into
   ¼-inch (6-mm) coins

¼ cup Chicken Stock
   (see page 225)

¼ teaspoon salt

⅛ teaspoon black pepper

Melt the butter, sugar and gingerroot together in a large sauté pan set on high heat. When the mixture begins to bubble and thicken, about 2 minutes, add the carrots. Cook for 2 minutes, until the carrots begin to release their juices. Add the chicken stock, cover and cook for 2 minutes. Remove the lid, stir in the salt and pepper and cook for 2-3 minutes longer, until most of the liquid has evaporated and the carrots are covered with a shiny glaze. Serve at once.

Carrots and Garlic

I want to say up front, the garlic is not overpowering, even if there are 20 cloves - try it and see!

Heat the butter, olive oil, sugar, garlic and thyme in a large sauté pan set on high heat. When the mixture begins to bubble and thicken, about 2 minutes, add the carrots. Cook for 2 minutes, until the carrots begin to release their juices. Add the chicken stock, cover and cook for 2 minutes. Remove the lid, stir in the salt and pepper and cook for 2-3 minutes longer, until most of the liquid has evaporated and the carrots are covered with a shiny glaze. Serve at once.

1 tablespoon butter

1 tablespoon olive oil

2 tablespoons sugar

20 garlic cloves, peeled and
    cut in half lengthwise

1 teaspoon thyme

1½ pounds (700 g) carrots,
    peeled and cut into
    ¼-inch (6-mm) coins

¼ cup Chicken Stock
    (see page 225)

¼ teaspoon salt

⅛ teaspoon black pepper

Pesto Peppers

So many flavors mingle during the baking of this rustic dish: sweet peppers, pesto, olives, and tomatoes. I also love the nice golden crust from the bread crumbs on top.

2 red bell peppers

1 tablespoon olive oil

3 Roma tomatoes, cut into
½-inch (1.5-cm) dice

3 tablespoons Pesto Sauce
(see page 82)

4 tablespoons chopped pitted
Greek or Sicilian
black olives

2 tablespoons Italian Bread
Crumbs (see page 230)

1 tablespoon freshly grated
Parmigiano Reggiano
cheese

Preheat the oven to 450° F (230° C). Grease an 8-inch (20-cm) square baking dish.

Cut the peppers in half through the stem - don't remove the stem. Remove the seeds and membrane and brush with the olive oil, inside and out. Place the pepper halves in the prepared baking dish, cut-side-up.

Toss the diced tomatoes with the pesto sauce. Fill the pepper halves with equal amounts of the tomatoes. Sprinkle the tops with the olives, bread crumbs and cheese. Bake for 30 minutes, until the upper edges are charred and blistered and the bread crumbs are golden brown. Serve hot or at room temperature.

Spinach with Raisins and Pine Nuts

S E R V E S   4

Sweet plump raisins, crunchy pine nuts and fresh spinach are a combination you'll want to cook again and again.

Bring the water to a boil in a large pot set on high heat. Add the spinach a little at a time, pushing it down to the bottom of the pot with a spoon. Give it a good stir once all the spinach has been added, reduce the heat to medium-high and cook for 10 minutes, stirring often. Drain well and set aside.

Heat the olive oil, pine nuts and garlic in a large sauté pan set on high heat until the garlic and pine nuts begin to brown, about 2-3 minutes. Drain the raisins, discarding the water. Add the spinach, raisins, salt and pepper to the pan and cook for 3-4 minutes, until heated through. Serve hot.

3 quarts (2.75 l) water

2 pounds (900 g) spinach leaves, washed and coarsely chopped

3 tablespoons olive oil

3 tablespoons pine nuts

4 garlic cloves, thickly sliced

5 tablespoons golden raisins, soaked in ½ cup hot water for 20 minutes

½ teaspoon salt

¼ teaspoon black pepper

Parsley New Potatoes

This is a very simple dish that is quite pretty with the red potato skins and the dark green parsley flecks. I've cooked it until just tender, so steam a few minutes longer if you like your potatoes really soft.

2 pounds (900 g) small
   red new potatoes, unpeeled
   and cut into quarters

3 tablespoons chopped fresh
   Italian parsley

2 tablespoons butter, melted

½ teaspoon salt

¼ teaspoon black pepper

Place about 2 inches (5 cm) of water in the bottom of a large pot. Set a steamer tray in the bottom, cover and bring to a boil. Place the potatoes in the steamer tray, cover the pot and steam for 12-15 minutes, until the potatoes are tender when pierced with a small knife. Transfer the potatoes to a bowl and toss with the remaining ingredients. Keep warm until ready to serve.

Potatoes au Gratin

My version of the French classic features thin slices of potatoes with a rich, cheesy garlic-spiked sauce. If you prepare it a day or two ahead of time, the flavors will deepen and make the dish even better.

Preheat the oven to 400° F (200° C). Grease a 9 x 13-inch (23 x 33-cm) baking dish with the butter. In a large bowl, toss the potatoes, salt, pepper and garlic. Spread one-third of the potatoes in the bottom of the baking dish. Top with 1 cup of the cheese, one-third of the potatoes, 1 cup of the cheese and the remaining potatoes. Pour the milk over the potatoes, cover the dish with foil and bake for 1 hour. Remove the foil and sprinkle the remaining cheese over the potatoes. Return to the oven for an additional 20 minutes, uncovered, until the top is toasty brown. Let the potatoes cool for 15-20 minutes before cutting into squares for serving.

½ tablespoon butter

3 pounds (1.4 kg) white potatoes, peeled and cut into very thin slices

1 teaspoon salt

½ teaspoon black pepper

6 garlic cloves, finely chopped

3 cups shredded Swiss cheese

3 cups milk or 1½ cups each milk and whipping cream

Twice-Baked Spinach Potatoes

Bright with color from the red tomato and green spinach, these potatoes have a nice creamy texture from the cheese. Prepare them a day ahead of time and finish baking with your main dish.

4 Russet potatoes

4 tablespoons butter, melted

6 tablespoons freshly grated
   Parmigiano Reggiano
   cheese

2 garlic cloves, finely chopped

¼ teaspoon salt

¼ teaspoon black pepper

½ cup chopped fresh spinach

¼ cup chopped tomatoes,
   preferably Roma

Preheat the oven to 400° F (200° C). Wash the potatoes and prick the skin on both sides with a fork. Place on a baking sheet and bake for 1 hour. Remove from the oven and cool for 10-15 minutes. When cool enough to handle, cut the potatoes in half, lengthwise. Scoop the pulp into a large mixing bowl, being careful not to tear the skin. Leave a ¼-inch (6-mm) thickness of pulp in the skin.

Preheat the oven to 400° F (200° C). Add 3 tablespoons of the butter, 4 tablespoons of the cheese, the garlic, salt and pepper to the potato pulp and mix well. Gently fold in the spinach and tomato. Fill the potato shells with the mixture, brush with the remaining butter and sprinkle with the remaining cheese. Place on a baking sheet and bake for 30 minutes, until the tops are browned. The twice-baked potatoes are ready to serve.

Roasted Potatoes with Pancetta and Onion

Here is a great dish for an autumn evening. Ask your produce manager for the sweetest onions to go with the smoky bacon.

Heat the olive oil in a large sauté pan set on medium-high heat until sizzling, about 2 minutes. Add the pancetta or bacon and cook for 3-4 minutes, until it's beginning to brown and the fat has been rendered. Remove the pancetta with a slotted spoon to a dish and set aside.

Preheat the oven to 425° F (220° C). In the same pan set on medium-high heat, toss the potatoes, salt and pepper, stirring until well coated with the oil. Cover the pan and cook for 10 minutes, stirring several times.

Transfer the potatoes to a baking sheet or a shallow roasting pan and roast for 20 minutes. Remove the pan from the oven and toss the potatoes. Sprinkle the reserved pancetta over the potatoes and top with the sliced onions. Return to the oven for an additional 20 minutes, stirring once or twice more. Serve hot.

1 tablespoon olive oil

1½ cups chopped or diced pancetta or thick bacon

2½ pounds (1.25 kg) baby red new potatoes with skin on, cut into quarters

¾ teaspoon salt

½ teaspoon black pepper

1 onion, cut into quarters and thinly sliced

Romano Mashed Potatoes

Romano is my favorite cheese. The sharp nutty flavor is a bit saltier than Parmesan cheese, so taste it before you add any additional salt. (Illustrated in the Entrées section.)

2 pounds (900 g) Russet
  potatoes, peeled and
  quartered

6 tablespoons freshly ground
  Pecorino Romano cheese

¼ teaspoon black pepper

¼ cup cream or milk

3 tablespoons chopped fresh
  Italian parsley

Put the potatoes into a large saucepan with enough water to cover by 2 inches (5 cm). Cover the pan and bring to a boil over high heat. Once the water reaches a boil, uncover, reduce the heat to medium-low and cook for 15-20 minutes, until the potatoes are so soft they will break with pressure from the back of a spoon. Drain well and return the potatoes to the pan. Add the cheese, black pepper, cream or milk and parsley and beat with an electric mixer until creamy. The potatoes are ready to serve.

Baked Onions

When the natural sugars from the onion juices bake with the balsamic vinegar, it reduces to a dense irresistible syrup. Do look for the sweetest onions possible for the best results. These onions will not make you cry!

Preheat the oven to 400°F (200°C). Put the onions and balsamic vinegar in an 8-inch (20-cm) square baking dish. Sprinkle with the salt and pepper. Top each onion with one-quarter of the butter. Cover the baking dish with aluminum foil and bake for 1 hour. Remove the foil, turn the onions over and cook for 30 minutes longer. Drizzle the onions with the pan juices and serve.

4 sweet onions, peeled, root and stem ends cut off

¼ cup balsamic vinegar

¼ teaspoon salt

⅛ teaspoon black pepper

1 tablespoon butter

Broiled Mushrooms and Onions

This is a simple dish with spectacular results. In fact, its warm, subtle flavors are so wonderful, it is addictive! It also tastes great the next day ... and the next ...

2 onions, cut in half lengthwise and cut crosswise into
   ½-inch (1.5-cm) slices

1 pound (450 g) mushrooms,
   stems trimmed and
   cut in half

4 tablespoons olive oil

½ teaspoon salt

¼ teaspoon black pepper

2 tablespoons lemon juice
   (optional)

¼ cup freshly grated
   Parmigiano Reggiano
   cheese

4 tablespoons chopped
   fresh basil

Preheat the broiler. Place the onions and mushrooms on a baking sheet in an even layer. Drizzle the olive oil evenly over the top and sprinkle with the salt and pepper. Place under the broiler, 4-6 inches (10-15 cm) from the heating element, and broil for 15-20 minutes, until the edges of the onions are browned and the mushrooms have started to release their juices. Halfway through the cooking time, give the vegetables a good stir. Place the vegetables in a shallow serving dish or bowl. Sprinkle with the lemon juice, if you wish, the cheese and the basil. Serve hot or at room temperature.

Braised Fennel

Fennel's licorice flavor is a favorite in the Mediterranean. Cooked this way, its flavor is quite subtle and has an almost creamy texture. The sauce is an extra step, but really looks and tastes wonderful.

Preheat the oven to 400° F (200° C). Cut the leafy stalks off the fennel bulbs. Trim the root ends - not too much, just enough to remove the brown from the end. You want enough of the root left to hold the pieces of fennel together. Cut or scrape away any brown spots from the outside of the fennel bulb. Cut each bulb lengthwise into quarters.

Mix the chicken stock and cream or milk in an 8-inch (20-cm) square baking dish. Place the fennel in the pan and sprinkle with the salt and pepper. Cover the pan with foil and bake for 45 minutes. Remove the foil and sprinkle with the cheese. Return to the oven and bake an additional 20 minutes. Drizzle the fennel with the pan juices and serve.

2 fennel bulbs

½ cup Chicken Stock (see page 225)

2 tablespoons whipping cream or milk

¼ teaspoon salt

⅛ teaspoon black pepper

¼ cup freshly grated Parmigiano Reggiano cheese

Cook's Tip

The pan juices can be turned into an elegant sauce by draining them into a small saucepan and bringing to a boil over medium-high heat. Remove the pan from the heat and stir in a slurry of 1½ teaspoons chicken stock mixed with 1½ teaspoons cornstarch. Return the pan to the heat and cook for 1-2 minutes, stirring occasionally, until thickened. Serve the sauce over the fennel or puddle it on the plate and top with the fennel to show off the nice browning of the cheese.

Chickpeas with Mint and Tomatoes

SERVES 4

Chickpeas dotted with red tomatoes are pretty, while the yogurt gives this dish a bright refreshing finish. Try it and let your palate taste the harmony of these flavors.

5 Roma tomatoes, cut into
   1-inch (2.5-cm) pieces

¼ teaspoon salt

¼ teaspoon black pepper

¼ teaspoon sugar

2 tablespoons olive oil

½ onion, thinly sliced

4 garlic cloves, thickly sliced

¼ teaspoon allspice

1 (15-ounce) (425-g) can
   chickpeas (garbanzo
   beans), drained

2 tablespoons chopped
   fresh mint

¼ cup plain yogurt

Combine the tomatoes, salt, pepper and sugar in a medium bowl. Let it sit for 5-10 minutes, until the tomatoes have released some of their juices.

Heat the olive oil in a large sauté pan set on high heat until sizzling, about 2 minutes. Add the onion, garlic and allspice. Cook for 1-2 minutes. Stir in the tomatoes and their juices and cook for 2 minutes. Add the chickpeas and mint and cook for 1-2 minutes to heat them through. Serve with the yogurt drizzled over the top.

Couscous Spinach Pilaf

Couscous is a Mediterranean grain that is so easy to prepare and so versatile, that you'll find many other ways to use it in your cooking. This version is a pretty golden color with dark green spinach flakes and a flash of lemon tang.

Heat the olive oil and garlic in a large sauté pan set on high heat until sizzling, about 2-3 minutes. Add the lemon zest and coriander and stir. Add the spinach. It will look like a lot of spinach when you first add it, but will wilt down quite fast, in about 2-3 minutes and begin to release its juices. Add the lemon juice, chicken stock, salt and pepper. Bring to a boil and stir in the couscous. Cover, remove from the heat and let sit for 5 minutes. Fluff the couscous with a fork and serve.

3 tablespoons olive oil

4 garlic cloves, thickly sliced

Zest of 1 lemon, grated

¾ teaspoon coriander

6 cups chopped fresh spinach

2 tablespoons lemon juice

1¼ cups Chicken Stock
  (see page 225)

1 teaspoon salt

½ teaspoon black pepper

1 (10-ounce) (300-g) box
  instant couscous

Rice Pilaf with Currants and Pine Nuts

SERVES 4

Tender rice, tossed with slightly sweet currants and crunchy pine nuts, makes a versatile combination that will complement many entrées. The addition of saffron or turmeric gives it a rich, warm golden color. (Illustrated in the Entrées section.)

2 tablespoons olive oil

½ cup finely chopped onion

2 garlic cloves, thickly sliced

1 bay leaf

¼ cup currants

¼ cup toasted pine nuts

⅛ teaspoon saffron powder
   or turmeric

¼ teaspoon cinnamon

½ teaspoon cumin

1 cup long-grain white rice

½ cup white wine

1½ cups Chicken Stock
   (see page 225)

¼ teaspoon salt

⅛ teaspoon black pepper

2 tablespoons chopped fresh
   mint or Italian parsley

Heat the olive oil in a large sauté pan set on medium-high heat until sizzling, about 2 minutes. Add the onion, garlic, bay leaf, currants, pine nuts, saffron or turmeric, cinnamon and cumin and cook for 3-4 minutes, until the onion is soft. Stir in the rice and cook for 2 minutes. Add ¼ cup of the white wine, stir to scrape up any browned bits from the pan bottom and cook for 1 minute, until the wine is absorbed. Stir in the remaining wine, the chicken stock, salt and pepper and bring to a boil. Cover the pan with a tight-fitting lid, reduce the heat to low and simmer for 20 minutes. Remove from the heat and let sit for 5 minutes. Stir the rice to fluff, remove the bay leaf and stir in the mint or parsley. The pilaf is ready to serve, but can be held for up to 15-20 minutes in the covered pan before serving.

Sardinian Cracker Bread

⌄

MAKES 10 (10-INCH) (25-CM) ROUNDS

Easy is the first word I think of in association with this bread. There's no yeast, no rising time and baking is minimal. The end result is dramatic, impressive looking and great to serve with the Mediterranean appetizer spreads. (Illustrated in the Appetizers section.)

Mix the flour and salt together in a large bowl. Gradually stir in the water, until a firm dough that isn't sticky starts to form. Turn out onto a lightly floured board and knead for a few minutes, until the dough is smooth.

Divide the dough into 10 balls. Place on a towel or work surface that has been sprinkled with flour. Let rest for 20-30 minutes.

Preheat the oven to 450° F (230° C). Place a baking sheet in the oven to preheat. On a lightly floured surface, roll each ball of dough out to a thickness of ¹⁄₁₆ inch (1.5 mm), about 10 inches (25 cm) in diameter.

Remove the hot baking sheet from the oven. Drape 1 of the circles of dough over the rolling pin and transfer it to the hot pan. Bake the bread for 2-3 minutes, then turn and bake for another 2-3 minutes. The bread should be flat and crisp, with many brown bubbles and browning at the edges. If it bends in the middle, even after cooling, it should go back in the oven to bake for a few minutes longer. (If the bread has puffed in the middle, like pita bread, then it was not rolled thin enough.) Remove the bread to a rack to cool and continue baking the other rounds on the preheated baking sheet, one at a time.

Store the bread in an airtight container or sealed storage bag for up to 2 weeks.

3½ cups all-purpose flour
1¼ teaspoons salt
1⅓ cups warm water

Cook's Tip

For a marvelous snack cracker, sprinkle the bread rounds with 1 tablespoon of freshly grated Parmigiano Reggiano cheese after turning it for the final baking.

Pita Bread

This is a Mediterranean classic whose simple, earthy qualities provide almost universal appreciation. Pita bread is now available in many grocery stores, but I assure you that the texture and flavor of fresh baked are far superior. Try it at least once to experience the difference. Because the rising times can't be rushed, start in the morning if you want to serve it in the evening.

1¼ teaspoons active dry yeast

2½ cups warm water

6 cups all-purpose flour

1½ teaspoons salt

½ tablespoon olive oil

Cornmeal for dusting the pans

Mix the yeast with 1¼ cups of the warm water and let sit to dissolve for a few minutes. Stir in 1½ cups of the flour, cover with a damp towel and place in a warm location for 4 hours to rise. The starter can rise overnight if you prefer starting it before you go to bed.

Stir the remaining warm water, the salt and 3½ cups of the flour into the starter. Stir or mix the dough with your hands until the consistency is thick and sticky. Sprinkle the remaining flour on a cutting board or work surface and turn the dough out onto it. Knead, incorporating the flour, until the consistency is smooth and elastic, about 10 minutes. Oil the bottom and sides of a large bowl with the olive oil. Place the dough in the bowl and cover with a damp towel. Let rise in a warm place for 1-1½ hours, or until doubled in size.

Preheat the oven to 425° F (220° C). Punch the dough down and divide into 8 equal pieces. Knead each piece on a floured board briefly to push out the air pockets, then form into balls. Using a rolling pin, roll each ball into an 8-inch (20-cm) diameter circle. If you have trouble getting the dough to roll out into a circle, simply cover the balls of dough with a damp cloth and let them rest for 15 minutes. It is important that the dough be rolled to a diameter of 8 inches (20 cm). If it is considerably less, the separation of the dough will be very uneven. If it is much more, the dough may not separate at all.

Place 2 of the circles of dough onto a large baking sheet that has been dusted with the cornmeal. Bake for 8-10 minutes, until puffed and golden brown. Remove from the oven, cover with a towel and let rest for 10 minutes. Push down on the bread to flatten and they're ready to serve. Store in plastic bags in the refrigerator for up to 10 days.

The versatility of this simple bread will give a whole new meaning to the expression "a pocket full of miracles."

Parmesan Nut Rolls

Small rolls have been popular in France since before the Middle Ages. The touch of honey mixed with Parmesan cheese makes these rolls both sweet and savory. Although there is very little "hands-on" time, you need to allow 2½ hours for the rising and baking time.

1 teaspoon sugar

1⅓-1½ cups warm water

1 envelope active dry yeast

4 cups unbleached
   all-purpose flour

1 teaspoon salt

⅔ cup freshly grated
   Parmigiano Reggiano
   cheese

2 tablespoons honey

¾ cup pine nuts
   or chopped walnuts

2 tablespoons olive oil

Mix the sugar with ¼ cup of the warm water in a glass measuring cup or bowl. Sprinkle in the yeast and set in a warm, draft-free place, for 10 minutes, until the yeast is foamy.

Combine the flour, salt and cheese in a large bowl. Make a well in the center and pour in the yeast mixture. Mix the honey with 1 cup of the remaining warm water and pour over the yeast mixture. Stir with a wooden spoon until the dry ingredients are evenly moistened, adding additional water if necessary. At this point, use your hands to work the dough into a ball. Remove the ball of dough from the bowl and knead on a lightly floured surface until smooth and elastic, about 5 minutes.

Place the dough in a lightly oiled bowl and cover with a damp cloth or plastic wrap. Set the bowl in a warm, draft-free place and let the dough rise until doubled in size, about 1½ hours.

Punch the dough down, flatten it out into a large rectangle and sprinkle with the nuts. Fold the bottom third of the dough up over the nuts, then the top third down over that. Knead for 3 minutes, to distribute the nuts throughout the dough.

Shape the dough into 12 small balls - don't make them perfectly round. Evenly space the rolls on a nonstick or lightly greased baking sheet. Cut an "X" into the top of each roll and brush with the olive oil. Set in a warm, draft-free place to rise for 20 minutes.

Preheat the oven to 400° F (200° C). Bake the rolls for 30 minutes until golden brown. Cool on a rack until ready to serve.

The trick to living happily
is learning to enjoy the small pleasures.
You can't wait for the big ones
because they don't come along often enough.
Fixing dinner is a readily available pleasure.
You can be creative, you can please someone else
and you can enjoy the food.

STANTON DELAPLANE

DESSERTS

The World is Big and Life is Short

*J*ust like all young boys, I found nothing more comforting than dessert if I was in the doldrums. Of course my mother, like mothers everywhere, understood the curative power a soft creamy scoop of Espresso Zabaglione or a slice of Chocolate Walnut Torte. She knew too well how she could change my gloomy mood with a little piece of Strawberry Tart or a serving of her famous Frozen Lemon Pistachio Cream. The memory of her homemade pies still makes my mouth water. Nobody could make a cake like Mom could ... except maybe for the bakers at Il Bar Del Viale.

It was at this famous open air cafe that I managed to put my weekly allowance to good use, sampling each of their delicacies. On many afternoons you could find me after school at one of the outdoor tables with a view of Via Della Liberta, Palermo's most fashionable boulevard. There was something more than just the food that attracted me to this cafe. It brought together two of my favorite things in life - good food and fascinating people. The street was alive with fashionable matrons patronizing the elegant neighborhood boutiques, young lovers strolling arm-in-arm, boys running up and down the sidewalk playing *Liberi Tutti*, a sort of tag game, and *gli anziani*, "the old people," walking their dogs. There was nothing more satisfying to the soul than sitting at one of these tables on a sunny afternoon, drinking espresso, devouring an apple flan and watching the world go by. *Ahh ... la dolce vita!* "Ahh ... the sweet life!" The master bakers at the cafe loved to experiment with all sorts of fancy desserts, introducing exotic foreign specialties like their little Greek pastries called Baklava, that quickly became the talk of the town. I loved these delicious phyllo dough pockets filled with a sweet mixture of almonds, brown sugar and butter. They never failed to work their restorative magic with me, no matter what.

Like the time I took my first girlfriend, Marillina, to Il Bar Del Viale. Before we even ordered our coffee, she told me it was over. As she walked away into the waiting arms of her new boyfriend, a loathsome college boy named Marco, my heart sank. Don Ciccio, one of the oldest waiters at the cafe, was watching the scene unfold. As I sat there feeling dejected and confounded, Don Ciccio quietly approached the table and placed a little dish of freshly baked baklava in front of me. "*U munnu è grandi,*" he said in his rich Sicilian dialect, "*e a vita è curta!*" "The world is big and life is short!" He smiled as he softly caressed the top of my head, then he walked away to leave me to find solace in the pastry. Holding back my tears, I lifted the baklava to my mouth. Suddenly, as the first taste of its sweet essence touched my tongue, I was transported. With each bite, my despondent gloom lifted and, in spite of myself, I smiled like the sun through a cloudy sky.

While I can't guarantee that a slice of my Walnut Cake or my favorite Cheesecake with Blackberry Sauce will solve the problems in your life, at least for a few moments it will bring a smile to your face and a little warmth into your heart.

Strawberries in Marsala with Sweetened Ricotta

SERVES 4 TO 6

You know from my television show that a splash of Marsala wine is one of my favorite taste sensations. You can get by without the alcohol if you desire; just add two more tablespoons of sugar to the strawberries. (Illustrated in this section.)

1 pound (450 g) strawberries,
   washed, hulled and
   quartered

2 tablespoons sugar

2 tablespoons sweet Marsala
   wine or orange liqueur

1¼ cups ricotta cheese

¼ cup mascarpone cheese
   or cream cheese

3 tablespoons honey

1 teaspoon vanilla

1 ounce (30 g) grated
   milk chocolate
   or semisweet chocolate

Mix the strawberries, sugar and Marsala or orange liqueur in a medium bowl and let sit for 30 minutes.

Combine the ricotta, mascarpone or cream cheese, honey and vanilla in another bowl, using an electric mixer or sturdy spoon to mix well. (This mixture can be prepared early in the day and refrigerated until 30 minutes before serving.)

Spoon the strawberries and their juices into individual bowls and top with the ricotta cheese. Sprinkle with the grated chocolate and serve.

Cook's Tip

For a more elegant presentation, use a pastry bag to pipe the ricotta mixture over the strawberries.

Espresso Zabaglione

The espresso makes this an invigorating variation of the classic Italian zabaglione. Light and fluffy, it's best when served immediately. (Illustrated in this section.)

In the top of a double boiler, whisk the egg yolks and sugar to a creamy consistency. In the bottom half of the double boiler, bring a small amount of water to the simmer. Place the egg mixture over the simmering water, making sure the bottom of the pan doesn't touch the water. Beat the mixture well with a whisk, until it begins to thicken, about 5 minutes. Be careful not to beat too long or you will cook the eggs.

Remove the top of the double boiler from the heat and whisk in the nutmeg, espresso and coffee liqueur. Return the pan to the double boiler and whisk until the mixture increases in volume and becomes light and fluffy, about 3-5 minutes. Remove from the heat and spoon the zabaglione into dessert dishes. Sprinkle with the grated chocolate and serve immediately.

4 egg yolks

¼ cup sugar

¼ teaspoon nutmeg

2 tablespoons strong coffee or 1½ teaspoons instant espresso powder dissolved in 2 tablespoons warm water

2 tablespoons coffee liqueur

½ cup grated semisweet chocolate

Cook's Tip

The zabaglione makes a great sauce spooned over ice cream. Don't forget to sprinkle grated semisweet chocolate on top!

Chocolate Zabaglione

Here is a great combination of chocolate, strawberry and vanilla. It's a fun way to serve zabaglione: a warm chocolate pudding-like sauce with cool ice cream and sweet strawberries - yummy!

2 ounces (60 g) semisweet chocolate

¼ cup whipping cream

4 egg yolks

4 tablespoons sugar

4 tablespoons sweet Marsala wine

1 quart (1 l) vanilla ice cream

2 cups fresh strawberries, sliced

Melt the chocolate and cream in a small saucepan set on low heat. Remove from the heat and set aside.

In the bottom half of a double boiler, bring a small amount of water to a simmer. In the top half of the double boiler, whisk the egg yolks and sugar to a creamy consistency. Place the egg mixture over the simmering water, making sure the bottom of the pan doesn't touch the water. Beat the mixture well with a whisk, until it begins to thicken, about 5 minutes. Be careful not to beat too long or you will cook the eggs. Remove from the heat and whisk in the Marsala. Return the pan to the top of the double boiler and whisk until the mixture increases in volume and becomes light and fluffy, about 3-5 minutes. Remove from the heat and fold in the chocolate mixture.

Scoop the ice cream into 8 dessert bowls. Top with the chocolate zabaglione and then the sliced strawberries. Serve immediately.

Cook's Tip

This thick, creamy zabaglione is an ideal dip for fruit. Spoon it into a serving bowl, place on a large platter or tray and surround with 1 quart (1 l) of fresh whole strawberries. Dip the strawberries into the zabaglione and enjoy!

OPPOSITE: (CLOCKWISE FROM TOP) ESPRESSO ZABAGLIONE (PAGE 183), CHOCOLATE ORANGE CREAM WITH RASPBERRIES (PAGE 185), STRAWBERRIES IN MARSALA WITH SWEETENED RICOTTA (PAGE 182).

Chocolate Orange Cream with Raspberries

Rich mascarpone cheese provides a voluptuous texture in this decadent dessert. It's also great to make ahead of time. (Illustrated in this section.)

In a medium bowl, toss the raspberries with the orange liqueur and sugar. Set aside.

Melt the chocolate in a small saucepan set on low heat, then whisk in the mascarpone cheese. Remove from the heat, stir in the orange zest and set aside.

Whip the cream in a large bowl with a whisk or electric mixer until stiff peaks form. (You have reached the stiff peak stage when you lift the whisk or beater from the cream and the top of the peak stands up straight.) Carefully fold the chocolate mixture into the whipped cream one-third at a time.

Spoon half the raspberries into 6 dessert dishes. Spoon the chocolate cream on top and sprinkle with the remaining raspberries. Serve immediately.

2 cups fresh berries, preferably raspberries

4 tablespoons Triple Sec or other orange-flavored liqueur

2 tablespoons sugar

3 ounces (90 g) semisweet chocolate

½ cup mascarpone cheese

1 tablespoon grated orange zest

1 cup whipping cream

OPPOSITE: ANISE TWISTS (PAGE 208). PREVIOUS PAGES, CLOCKWISE FROM TOP: BAKLAVA (PAGE 205), STRAWBERRY TART (PAGE 201), COFFEE CHEESECAKE (PAGE 198).

Apricot Peach Cream

This dessert is called a "cream" because of its seductive silky texture. Its intense orange color is beautiful on top of vanilla ice cream or swirled with vanilla yogurt.

3 (16-ounce) (450-g) cans
   peaches in light syrup

½ cup water

1 cup dried apricots

1 teaspoon vanilla

1 tablespoon honey

1 tablespoon lemon juice

1 egg

Drain the peach syrup into a small saucepan. Reserve the peaches separately and set aside. Add the water and the apricots to the peach syrup and simmer on low heat for 1 hour to soften the apricots. Drain and discard the liquid. Transfer the apricots to a food processor or blender with the remaining ingredients. Process until completely smooth. Pour into a large saucepan set on medium heat and cook for 7 minutes, stirring. Don't let the mixture come to a boil - it simply needs to get hot enough to thicken slightly and cook the egg.

Pour into 8 small dessert cups or bowls and refrigerate for at least 2 hours or overnight. Serve chilled.

Honey Orange Mousse

Here is a frozen dessert with the texture of light whipped ice cream. It's perfect served with your favorite ripe fresh fruit.

With an electric mixer, beat the egg yolks and honey in a large bowl until very thick, about 8-10 minutes. Stir in the nutmeg and orange zest. In a separate bowl, beat the cream until soft peaks form. Fold the whipped cream into the honey mixture.

Spoon the mousse into 8 small (¾ cup) custard cups. Cover the dishes with plastic wrap and freeze for 2-3 hours or overnight. Remove from the freezer 15-20 minutes before serving and let sit at room temperature to soften the texture.

6 egg yolks

⅓ cup honey

⅛ teaspoon nutmeg

2 teaspoons grated orange zest

1 cup heavy cream

Mascarpone Coffee Whip with Chocolate Sauce

SERVES 4 TO 6

Easy and elegant, this dessert can be made a few days ahead of time. Just drizzle with the chocolate sauce before serving.

CHOCOLATE SAUCE

½ cup whipping cream

4 ounces (115 g) semisweet chocolate chips

¼ cup corn syrup

Pinch of salt

MASCARPONE COFFEE WHIP

½ cup mascarpone cheese

2 tablespoons coffee liqueur

2 teaspoons instant espresso powder dissolved in 2 teaspoons warm water

¼ teaspoon ground nutmeg

2 tablespoons sugar

1 cup whipping cream

For the Chocolate Sauce, combine the cream and chocolate chips in a small saucepan set on medium heat, stirring until the chocolate has melted. Stir in the corn syrup and salt. Set aside.

For the Mascarpone Coffee Whip, combine the mascarpone cheese, coffee liqueur, espresso powder mixture, nutmeg and sugar in a medium bowl, using a whisk or rubber spatula to mix well.

In another bowl, whip the cream with a whisk or electric mixer until stiff peaks form. Fold the cream into the cheese mixture one-third at a time. Spoon or pipe (using a pastry bag) the mixture into individual dessert dishes. Drizzle with the chocolate sauce.

Cook's Tip

Another topping that adds a delightful crunch to this dessert is crumbled Amaretti cookies or Orange Almond Biscotti (page 207). Simply crumble one Amaretti cookie per serving or one biscotti for two servings. Sprinkle over the dessert after it has been drizzled with the chocolate sauce.

188 MEDITERRANEAN FLAVORS

Italian Mocha Cream Pudding

Italy has innumerable versions of these "cooked creams" that are known as pannacotta. This version's perfect balance of coffee and chocolate give it that popular mocha flavor. It's a very simple preparation, using gelatin instead of egg yolks, for a rich, creamy texture.

In a small dish, sprinkle the gelatin powder over the cold water. Let it sit for 10 minutes to soften the gelatin.

In the bottom half of a double boiler, bring a small amount of water to a simmer. Melt the chocolate, ½ cup of the whipping cream, the sugar and espresso powder in the top of the double boiler, stirring well. Make sure the chocolate has melted completely and that the mixture doesn't look grainy - it should be thick and shiny. Slowly whisk in the remaining cream and the milk. Heat just until steaming - do not boil. Stir in the softened gelatin and the vanilla, stirring just until the gelatin is completely dissolved.

Pour the mixture into 8 small custard cups or dessert molds. Chill in the refrigerator for 4-5 hours or overnight.

To serve, dip the custard cups or molds in a bowl of hot water for 20-30 seconds to loosen the edges. Turn out onto small serving dishes and garnish with the fresh berries and a sprig of the mint, if you wish.

1 envelope unflavored gelatin

2 tablespoons cold water

⅓ cup semisweet chocolate chips

1¾ cups whipping cream

6 tablespoons sugar

3 tablespoons instant espresso powder

1½ cups milk

2 teaspoons vanilla

Fresh berries for decoration (optional)

Mint sprigs for decoration (optional)

Strawberry Meringues

These slow-baked cookies look like white clouds with red strawberry polka dots. They're great with coffee or tea and just plain fun to eat.

2 egg whites

1 cup powdered sugar

¼ cup finely chopped
    fresh strawberries

Preheat the oven to 250° F (120° C). Grease and flour a large (13 x 18-inch) (33 x 46-cm) cookie sheet. Put the cookie sheet inside another cookie sheet of the same size to prevent the meringues from browning too much on the bottom. Set aside.

Whip the egg whites at low speed with an electric mixer until they look foamy, about 2 minutes. Increase the speed to high and continue beating until soft peaks form, about 1½ minutes. Gradually beat in the sugar. The whites will become very creamy and glossy, with stiff peaks forming, in 5-6 minutes. Gently fold in the chopped strawberries.

Drop tablespoons of the meringue, about 2 inches (5 cm) in diameter, on the prepared cookie sheet 1 inch (2.5 cm) apart. Bake for 1 hour, until firm on the outside. The inside will still be a little moist and the outside should be light in color. Remove from the oven and cool on the cookie sheet for 10 minutes.

Loosen the meringues with a spatula and transfer them to a serving plate. The meringues may be stored at room temperature, lightly covered with plastic wrap, for up to 3 days.

Frozen Lemon Pistachio Cream

In Italy, this popular dessert is called a semifreddo. In this version, the luscious lemon cream has an irresistible subtle crunch from the pistachio nuts.

The day before serving, grease a standard loaf pan (4½ x 8-inches) (11.5 x 20-cm). Line the pan with plastic wrap, leaving a 2-inch (5-cm) overhang on the short ends. Grease the plastic wrap with butter. Sprinkle 6 tablespoons of the ½ cup of chopped pistachios over the bottom and sides of the pan and set aside.

Beat the egg yolks, ⅓ cup of the sugar and the vanilla in a small bowl with an electric mixer until the mixture is thick enough to form a long ribbon when you lift the beaters, about 3 minutes. Add the mascarpone or cream cheese, beat for 2 minutes and set aside.

Clean the beaters carefully. In a clean bowl, beat the egg whites with the remaining sugar until they form stiff peaks and have a glossy sheen, about 3 minutes. Fold the egg whites into the cheese mixture, one-third at a time, then fold in the ⅓ cup of pistachios and the lemon zest. Pour the custard mixture into the prepared pan, sprinkle the remaining 2 tablespoons of pistachios over the top and cover with plastic wrap. Freeze overnight.

The day of serving, remove the frozen custard from the freezer and peel the plastic wrap away from the top of the custard. Turn the frozen custard out onto a platter and remove the plastic wrap. Cut into slices 1-1½ inches (2.5-4 cm) thick and serve immediately.

The pistachio cream will keep up to 2 months in the freezer.

½ cup + ⅓ cup finely chopped toasted pistachios

4 eggs, separated

⅔ cup sugar

1 teaspoon vanilla

8 ounces (225 g) mascarpone cheese or cream cheese

4 teaspoons grated lemon zest

Frozen Cappuccino Cream

The rich coffee flavor of this mousse-like cream is perfectly complemented by crunchy hazelnuts.

½ cup finely chopped
   toasted hazelnuts

4 eggs, separated

⅔ cup sugar

1 tablespoon instant espresso
   powder or instant coffee
   powder mixed with
   1 teaspoon warm water

8 ounces (225 g) mascarpone
   cheese or cream cheese

The day before serving, grease a standard loaf pan (4½ x 8-inches) (11.5 x 20-cm). Line the pan with plastic wrap, leaving a 2-inch (5-cm) overhang on the ends. Grease the plastic wrap with butter. Sprinkle 6 tablespoons of the chopped hazelnuts over the bottom and sides of the pan and set aside.

Beat the egg yolks, ⅓ cup of the sugar and the espresso mixture in a small bowl with an electric mixer until the mixture is thick enough to form a long ribbon when you lift the beaters, about 3 minutes. Add the mascarpone or cream cheese, beat for 2 minutes and set aside.

Clean the beaters carefully. In a clean bowl, beat the egg whites with the remaining sugar until they form stiff peaks and have a glossy sheen, about 3 minutes. Fold the egg whites into the cheese mixture, one-third at a time. Pour the custard mixture into the prepared pan, sprinkle the remaining hazelnuts over the top and cover with plastic wrap. Freeze overnight.

The day of serving, remove the frozen custard from the freezer and peel the plastic wrap away from the top of the custard. Turn the frozen custard out onto a platter and remove the plastic wrap. Cut into slices 1-1½ inches (2.5-4 cm) thick and serve immediately.

The cappuccino cream will keep up to 2 months in the freezer.

Apple Flan with Cinnamon Caramel Sauce

Flans have been a favorite Spanish dessert for centuries. In this version, I love the striking contrast of the cream-colored apple custard with the dark cinnamon syrup.

For the Cinnamon Caramel Sauce, combine 1 cup of the sugar and ⅓ cup of the water in a medium saucepan set on medium-high heat. Bring to a boil, swirling the pan over the heat to dissolve the sugar - don't stir the mixture. Cover the pan tightly and boil for 4-5 minutes, until the bubbles are thick and large. Uncover and continue boiling, swirling the pan constantly in a circular motion. Once the color begins to darken, continue to cook for approximately 1 minute longer, until light brown in color. Remove from the heat and keep swirling the pan, as the caramel will continue to darken from the heat in the pan. Add the cinnamon and swirl to mix it into the caramel. Pour the caramel into a 2-quart (2-l) round glass baking dish that is approximately 8-9 inches (20-23 cm) wide at the top, turning to coat the bottom and halfway up the sides with the caramel. Set aside.

For the Apple Flan, preheat the oven to 350° F (180° C). Bring the 5 cups of water to a boil and keep at a simmer until needed. In a medium bowl, whisk together the egg yolks, eggs and the sugar. Stir in the half-and-half milk, applesauce and vanilla. Pour into the caramel-coated bowl and set the bowl of custard into a 9 x 13-inch (23 x 33-cm) baking dish. Place the custard in the oven and pour the boiling water into the larger baking dish. Bake for 1½ hours, until the edges are just set and the center is still slightly liquid. Remove from the oven and cool for 15 minutes. Cover and refrigerate for at least 2 hours or overnight.

To unmold, place the baking dish in a pan of hot water for 1 minute to soften the caramel. Place a serving plate over the custard and invert the 2 dishes. Cut into wedges and drizzle with some of the sauce before serving.

CINNAMON CARAMEL SAUCE

1 cup sugar

⅓ cup water

½ teaspoon cinnamon

APPLE FLAN

5 cups water

3 egg yolks

3 eggs

½ cup sugar

1½ cups half-and-half milk

1 cup unsweetened applesauce

1 teaspoon vanilla

Honey Vanilla Rice Flan

The basic Spanish flan can be the starting point for great personal creativity. In this version, the flan becomes an elegant rice pudding, flavored with the delicate sweetness of honey.

1 cup sugar

⅓ cup + 5 cups water

⅓ cup short grain rice,
    preferably arborio

1½ cups milk

1 cup half-and-half milk

1 tablespoon vanilla

3 eggs

3 egg yolks

⅓ cup honey

Stir the sugar and the ⅓ cup of water together in a medium saucepan. Cook the caramel sauce as directed on page 193. Pour the caramel into a 2-quart (2-l) round glass baking dish that is approximately 8-9 inches (20-23 cm) wide at the top, turning to coat the bottom and halfway up the sides with the caramel. Set aside.

Preheat the oven to 350° F (180° C). Bring the 5 cups of water to a boil and keep at a simmer until needed. In a medium saucepan set on medium-high heat, bring the rice, milk and half-and-half to a simmer. Cook for 10 minutes, stirring frequently. Mix together the vanilla, eggs, egg yolks and honey in a medium bowl. Slowly pour a small amount of the hot milk mixture into the egg mixture, stirring constantly. Pour the egg mixture into the milk in the saucepan and mix well. Cook over medium heat for 5-10 minutes, until the custard becomes slightly thickened, stirring to prevent sticking.

Pour the custard into the prepared dish, then place the dish into a 9 x 13-inch (23 x 33-cm) baking dish. Place the custard in the oven and pour the boiling water into the larger baking dish. Bake for 40 minutes, until the edges are just set and the center is still slightly liquid.

Remove the custard from the oven and cool for 15 minutes before serving. If you prefer to serve the flan cold, cover and refrigerate for at least 2 hours or overnight. To serve, place the bowl in a pan of hot water for 1 minute to soften the caramel before unmolding onto a serving plate. Cut into wedges.

Lemon Soufflé

I have given my version of the basic French soufflé a bright lemon flavor and used a very small amount of flour to give it the lightest texture possible. Serve it with blackberry sauce (page 196) for a stunning contrast in both appearance and flavor.

Preheat the oven to 400° F (200° C). Butter a 6-cup soufflé dish. Sprinkle a little granulated sugar into the dish and roll it around to coat the bottom and sides.

In a medium saucepan, whisk the half-and-half and the flour, until smooth. Stir in the lemon juice, lemon zest and sugar. Cook, stirring constantly, over medium heat until thickened and smooth, about 5 minutes. Remove from the heat and set aside.

In a large bowl, beat the egg whites and salt until stiff peaks form. (Egg whites beat to the greatest volume when they are at room temperature.)

Whisk the egg yolks and vanilla into the milk mixture, one at a time. Fold the egg whites into the milk/yolk mixture, one-third at a time. Pour into the prepared soufflé dish and bake for 10 minutes. Reduce the oven temperature to 350° F (180° C). Bake for 20-25 minutes, until puffy and golden brown. Dust with the powdered sugar and serve immediately.

½ cup half-and-half milk

3 tablespoons flour

¼ cup freshly squeezed lemon juice

2 teaspoons grated lemon zest

½ cup sugar

6 egg whites, at room temperature

Pinch of salt

4 egg yolks

½ teaspoon vanilla

1 tablespoon powdered sugar

Cheesecake with Blackberry Sauce

⌄

SERVES 8 TO 10

Everyone in the world asks me for cheesecake recipes, and this is one of the creamiest versions you'll ever make! Flavored with honey and orange-flower water, it provides a delightful surprise to your palate. It you can't find orange-flower water, 2 teaspoons of orange zest will do just fine. The blackberry sauce is quite simple to make and can be done while the cheesecake is baking.

WALNUT-AMARETTI CRUST

4 tablespoons flour
1 cup ground Amaretti cookies
   (about 26 cookies)
1½ cups ground walnuts
6 tablespoons unsalted butter,
   melted
⅛ teaspoon salt

ORANGE CREAM CHEESE FILLING

1½ pounds (700 g)
   cream cheese, at
   room temperature
½ cup honey
1 teaspoon orange-flower
   water
1 tablespoon brandy
   or 1 teaspoon brandy
   extract
3 eggs

BLACKBERRY SAUCE MAKES 1 CUP

8 ounces (225 g)
   frozen blackberries
1 tablespoon lemon juice
¼ cup sugar
3 tablespoons water

For the Walnut-Amaretti Crust, mix together all the crust ingredients. Press into a 9-inch (23-cm) springform pan, patting the mixture evenly over the bottom and two-thirds of the way up the sides of the pan.

Preheat the oven to 325° F (170° C). To prepare the Orange Cream Cheese Filling, beat the cream cheese with an electric mixer until fluffy, about 2 minutes. Beat in the honey, orange-flower water and brandy. Add the eggs, one at a time, beating well after each addition. Pour the batter into the prepared crust and bake for 1¼ hours, or until a knife inserted in the center comes out clean. Remove from the oven and cool completely on a baking rack. Cover and refrigerate for at least 4 hours or overnight.

To serve the cheesecake, remove it from the refrigerator and take off the side ring. Place on a serving dish and cut into wedges. Serve each slice drizzled with the blackberry sauce.

For the Blackberry Sauce, put all the ingredients in a small saucepan set on medium heat. Simmer for 5 minutes, until the berries are thawed and have broken up. Put the mixture into a food processor or blender and process for 1 minute. Pour through a fine sieve to remove the solids. Discard the solids and place the sauce in a covered container. Refrigerate until needed.

Cook's Tip

The blackberry sauce is great to have on hand for topping ice cream, pound cake or fresh fruit. It will keep up to 2 weeks in the refrigerator or can be frozen in ice cube trays, transferred to freezer bags and stored up to 3 months. Thaw as needed in the microwave oven or a small saucepan on the stove top.

Everyone has his weakness and this is mine. When it comes to this dessert, I simply can't say no.

Coffee Cheesecake

⌄

SERVES 8 TO 10

Forget about your diet once in a while. Let the buttery chocolate crust, filled with creamy coffee cheese filling, take you to a world of culinary delights. (Illustrated in this section.)

CHOCOLATE GRAHAM
CRACKER CRUST

1¾ cups crushed chocolate
   graham crackers

½ cup (1 stick) butter, melted

⅛ teaspoon salt

COFFEE CREAM
CHEESE FILLING

1½ pounds (700 g)
   cream cheese, at
   room temperature

1 cup sugar

3 eggs

¾ cup whipping cream

2 teaspoons vanilla

3 tablespoons instant espresso
   powder dissolved in
   ¼ cup warm water

Whipped cream (optional)

Nutmeg (optional)

Preheat the oven to 325° F (170° C). For the Chocolate Graham Cracker Crust, mix all the ingredients in a medium bowl. Pat the mixture evenly over the bottom and 1½ inches (4 cm) up the sides of a 9-inch (23-cm) springform pan. Set aside.

For the Coffee Cream Cheese Filling, beat the cream cheese and sugar with an electric mixer until light and fluffy, about 2 minutes. Add the eggs, one at a time, beating well after each addition. Reduce the speed to low and add the cream, vanilla and espresso, one at a time, blending well after each addition.

Pour the batter into the prepared crust and bake for 1½ hours, until puffed around the edges. The center will still look soft and jiggly. Chill for at least 4 hours or overnight.

Serve with a dollop of the whipped cream and a sprinkle of the nutmeg, if you wish.

Cook's Tip

To make cutting the cheesecake easier, dip a knife into hot water before cutting the slices.

Ricotta Raisin Tart

I think of this dessert as a luscious cheesecake, dotted with plump, rum-soaked raisins, and the added benefit of a tender buttery crust! It's a very popular tart that is featured prominently in bakeries throughout Rome.

In a small bowl, soak the raisins in the rum for ½ hour. Drain, reserving the raisins and 2 tablespoons of the rum separately. Set aside.

Prepare the pie dough. Partially bake the tart shell as directed (see page 232) using a 9-inch (23-cm) tart pan with a removable bottom. Set aside.

Preheat the oven to 350° F (180° C). In a large bowl, beat the sugar and egg with an electric mixer, until creamy. Add the cream cheese and beat until well incorporated. Beat in the ricotta cheese. Stir in all but 3 tablespoons of the soaked raisins and the reserved rum. Pour the cheese mixture into the partially baked tart shell and sprinkle with the reserved raisins. Bake for 25-30 minutes, until the center doesn't jiggle when the pan is moved. Remove from the oven and cool to room temperature before serving.

½ cup raisins

¼ cup dark rum (see Cook's Tip)

½ recipe Pie Dough, partially baked (see page 232)

¼ cup sugar

1 egg

4 ounces (115 g) cream cheese, at room temperature

1 cup ricotta cheese

Cook's Tip

If you don't have rum, plump the raisins in warm water for 30 minutes. Drain the soaking water and discard. Use ¼ teaspoon of rum extract in place of the 2 tablespoons of rum in the filling.

Pine Nut Tart

The golden-brown pine nuts nestled in their buttery crust make a striking presentation. It is a delightful Mediterranean version of the American favorite, pecan pie.

½ recipe Pie Dough,
   partially baked
   (see page 232)

¼ cup apricot jam
   or preserves

2 eggs

¼ cup sugar

1 teaspoon vanilla

⅛ teaspoon salt

½ cup mascarpone cheese

1 cup toasted pine nuts

Prepare the pie dough. Partially bake the tart shell as directed (see page 232) using a 9-inch (23-cm) tart pan with a removable bottom. Cool at room temperature on a baking rack. Spread the jam or preserves over the bottom of the cooled tart shell. Set aside.

Preheat the oven to 350° F (180° C). In a large bowl, combine the eggs, sugar, vanilla and salt, stirring until smooth and creamy. Add the mascarpone cheese and mix well. Stir in the pine nuts. Pour the mixture into the prepared tart shell and bake for 30 minutes, until the top is a golden brown. Remove from the oven and cool on a baking rack for 10-15 minutes. Serve warm or at room temperature.

Strawberry Tart

First off, I recommend always making two of these tarts because one will not last long. Its appeal is due in part to the combination of strawberries over a layer of almonds. (Illustrated in this section.)

Prepare the pie dough. Partially bake the tart shell as directed (see page 232) using a 9-inch (23-cm) tart pan with a removable bottom. Reserve the remaining half of the pie dough.

Combine the strawberries, sugar and 2 tablespoons of the flour in a medium saucepan. Stir over medium heat until the sugar is dissolved and the mixture is thickened, about 5-10 minutes. Set aside.

Preheat the oven to 350° F (180° C). In a small bowl, mix the butter, powdered sugar, ground almonds, the remaining flour and the almond extract. The mixture will be crumbly. Sprinkle the almond mixture over the prepared tart shell. Pour the strawberries on top and spread evenly.

Roll out the reserved pie dough to a 10-inch (25-cm) circle and cut into ½-inch (1.5-cm) wide strips. Lay half the strips of dough across the tart 1 inch (2.5 cm) apart. Lay the remaining strips across those, forming a lattice pattern. Press the ends of the strips onto the edge of the tart shell and trim away the excess dough. Bake for 35 minutes or until the lattice top is golden brown. Remove from the oven and cool on a baking rack. Serve warm or at room temperature.

1 recipe Pie Dough,
   partially baked
   (see page 232)

2 cups sliced fresh strawberries

½ cup sugar

6 tablespoons all-purpose flour

2 tablespoons butter, melted

2 tablespoons powdered sugar

¼ cup ground almonds

¼ teaspoon almond extract

Apricot Tart

Glowing golden apricots make this tart shine like a stained glass window. But don't just look at it - you'll also love tasting the creaminess from the honey-sweetened cream cheese. This is a good dessert to make at the last minute, because you may already have all the ingredients in your cupboard.

½ recipe Pie Dough
    (see page 232)

¾ cup water

3 tablespoons honey

6 ounces (175 g)
    dried apricots

4 ounces (115 g) cream cheese

2 tablespoons chopped
    pistachios or walnuts

Prepare the pie dough and bake the tart shell as directed (see page 232) using a 9-inch (23-cm) tart pan with a removable bottom. Cool at room temperature on a baking rack and set aside.

Bring the water, 1 tablespoon of the honey and the apricots to a boil in a small saucepan set on medium-high heat. Cover, reduce the heat to low and simmer for 15 minutes. Remove from the heat, uncover and cool for 15 minutes. Purée the apricots and their liquid in a food processor or blender for 2 minutes, until a smooth, spreadable consistency is reached.

Using an electric hand mixer, beat the cream cheese and the remaining honey to a spreadable consistency. Spread the cream cheese over the bottom of the pre-baked tart shell. Pour the puréed apricots over the cream cheese and smooth with a spatula. Sprinkle the chopped nuts over the tart. Cover and chill for 2 hours before serving.

Serve cold or warm at room temperature for 30 minutes before serving.

Plum Tart in Phyllo Pastry

Phyllo dough is a great Mediterranean product that cooks into a crisp flaky crust. The plum quarters make a lovely presentation, but do experiment with the fruit of your choice.

Preheat the oven to 375°F (190°C). Brush the bottom of a 9-inch (23-cm) fluted tart pan with a removable bottom with some of the melted butter.

Brush each of the 6 sheets of phyllo with the melted butter. (Be sure to save 2 tablespoons of the melted butter for drizzling over the filled tart.) Fold each sheet of phyllo in half by bringing the short sides together. Place 2 of the folded sheets in the prepared pan, side-by-side, with the folded sides slightly overlapping in the center of the pan. Place 2 more sheets of phyllo on top, so their seam is going the opposite direction. Place the last 2 phyllo sheets on top, arranging them so they are slightly overlapping and so their seam does not line up with the others. Roll the overlapping edges of the phyllo up and press into the sides of the pan to form an attractive edge for the crust. Brush the surface and sides with the melted butter and then a little of the beaten egg white. Bake for 5 minutes and remove from the oven. The top layer of phyllo may have puffed up a bit, but just push it back down. Don't worry if it crumbles a little.

Arrange the plum quarters in the phyllo crust in concentric circles. Drizzle with the remaining 2 tablespoons of melted butter and sprinkle with the sugar. Bake for 45 minutes, until the pastry is golden brown. Cool for 10-15 minutes on a baking rack. Serve warm or at room temperature.

6 sheets frozen phyllo pastry, thawed

4 tablespoons butter, melted

1 egg white, lightly beaten

1 pound (450 g) plums, quartered and pitted

2 tablespoons sugar

Cook's Tip

Don't make this dessert too far in advance, or the dough will become soggy from the plum juices. You can always crisp it up at 325°F (170°C) for 10 minutes and serve warm.

Apricot Raspberry Clafouti

This French dessert is a cross between a custard and a pancake. It has a dramatic appearance, bursting with apricot and raspberry flavor. By using canned or frozen fruit, you can make it all year round.

2 tablespoons butter

¾ cup all-purpose flour

3 eggs

1 cup milk

2 teaspoons vanilla

¼ teaspoon salt

¾ cup sugar

2 (15-ounce) (425-g) cans
   apricot halves in heavy
   syrup, drained and
   syrup discarded

½ cup frozen raspberries

Preheat the oven to 375° F (190° C). Melt the butter in a 10-inch (25-cm) pie pan or 1½-quart (1.5-l) shallow baking dish.

In a food processor or blender, combine the flour, eggs, milk, vanilla, salt and ½ cup of the sugar. Process until the batter is well mixed, about 30 seconds.

Swirl the melted butter around the pan to coat the sides and bottom completely. Pour the batter into the pan. Arrange the apricot halves, round-side-up, on top. Top evenly with the raspberries. Sprinkle with the remaining sugar and bake for 45-55 minutes, until golden brown and puffy. The clafouti will fall a bit after it is removed from the oven.

Cut into wedges and serve warm or at room temperature.

Baklava

T his might be the most famous Eastern Mediterranean pastry in the world. In my version, layers of flaky phyllo dough are drizzled with honey syrup and crunchy walnuts. The frozen phyllo dough makes it especially easy to prepare. (Illustrated in this section.)

For the Cinnamon Syrup, combine the sugar, honey, water, lemon juice and cinnamon stick, if you wish, in a medium saucepan set on medium-high heat. Bring to a boil, stirring to dissolve the sugar. Reduce the heat to low and simmer for 10 minutes, until thickened. Remove from the heat and stir in the orange-flower water or rosewater. Set aside for 10 minutes to cool, then refrigerate until needed.

For the Honey-Nut Pastry, combine the nuts, sugar and cinnamon (if using) in a medium bowl. Set aside.

Lay the phyllo sheets on a flat surface and cover with a lightly dampened towel. Lightly grease a 9 x 13-inch (23 x 33-cm) baking pan with some of the melted butter. Brush half a sheet of phyllo with melted butter, then fold in half by bringing the short sides together. Brush the top half of the same sheet with butter, then place in the greased pan. Repeat with 4 more sheets of phyllo, then top with one-third of the nut mixture. Repeat the layers of phyllo and nuts, ending with a layer of phyllo. Brush the top liberally with melted butter, then cover and refrigerate for 15 minutes.

Preheat the oven to 350°F (180°C). Remove the baklava from the refrigerator. With a sharp knife, make lengthwise cuts 1 inch (2.5 cm) apart, cutting all the way through to the bottom. Cut diagonally across the lengthwise cuts to make diamonds. Bake for 30-35 minutes, then reduce the heat to 300°F (150°C) and bake for 15 minutes longer, until the top is crisp and golden brown. Remove from the oven and immediately pour the cool syrup over the top. Let cool completely, then cut over the same lines again before serving. The baklava may be prepared several days ahead.

CINNAMON SYRUP

1¼ cups sugar

¼ cup honey

¾ cup water

4 tablespoons lemon juice

1 (3-inch) (8-cm) cinnamon stick (optional)

2 tablespoons orange-flower water or rosewater (optional)

HONEY-NUT PASTRY

2 cups coarsely ground walnuts or almonds or half of each

3 tablespoons brown sugar

½ teaspoon cinnamon (optional)

20 sheets frozen phyllo pastry, thawed

1 cup (2 sticks) butter, melted and foam skimmed from top

Crunchy Hazelnut Shortbread

The texture of this cake is more like a shortbread cookie with a crunchy praline topping. It's a rustic dessert - casually break it into chunks as opposed to trying to cut it into elegant even pieces. You'll find it's great for sharing with friends and children will love it!

1¼ cups brown sugar

1 cup whole hazelnuts

1½ cups (3 sticks) butter

1 teaspoon vanilla

1½ teaspoons salt

3 cups all-purpose flour

½ cup chopped hazelnuts

Preheat the oven to 325° F (170° C). Line the bottom and sides of a 9 x 13-inch (23 x 33-cm) baking pan with aluminum foil. Lightly butter the foil. Evenly sprinkle ¾ cup of the brown sugar and the whole hazelnuts over the bottom of the pan.

In a large bowl, beat the butter, the remaining brown sugar, vanilla and salt with an electric mixer, until light and fluffy. Beat in the flour and the chopped hazelnuts at low speed, until the mixture begins to cling to the beaters. Scatter the dough over the sugar and nuts in the bottom of the prepared pan and press it into an even layer with your fingers.

Bake for 30 minutes, until the top is lightly browned. Cool for 10 minutes on a rack. Top with a cutting board or serving plate and invert. Remove the foil carefully and cut into squares while still warm. (The cake is very crumbly, so don't worry about cutting even pieces.) Serve warm or at room temperature.

Orange Almond Biscotti

MAKES 4½ DOZEN COOKIES

One taste and you'll know why biscotti is the most famous cookie of southern Italy! Biscotti have an irresistible crunchy texture that comes from baking them twice - perfect for dipping into coffee or dessert wine. This recipe makes a lot of cookies, but they store beautifully.

Preheat the oven to 325° F (170° C). Grease and flour a large baking sheet. Sift together the flour, baking powder, baking soda and salt. Set aside.

Beat the eggs and sugar in a large bowl with an electric mixer, until light and creamy. Beat in the orange zest and almond extract. Stir in the dry ingredients, then the almonds.

Divide the dough in half and shape into 2 (14 x 1½-inch) (35 x 4-cm) logs, smoothing the tops and sides with a rubber spatula. Place the logs about 4 inches (10 cm) apart on the baking sheet and bake for 30 minutes, or until firm and golden brown. Remove the logs from the oven and let cool for 10 minutes. Reduce the oven heat to 275° F (135° C).

Transfer the logs to a cutting board and cut diagonally into ½-inch (1.5-cm) slices, using a serrated knife. Stand the slices vertically on end about ½ inch (1.5 cm) apart on the baking sheet. Bake for 30 minutes. Transfer to wire racks to cool. The biscotti will keep in a tightly sealed container for 3-4 weeks.

2½ cups all-purpose flour

1 teaspoon baking powder

½ teaspoon baking soda

1 teaspoon salt

4 eggs

¾ cup sugar

4 teaspoons grated orange zest

1 teaspoon almond extract

1 cup whole toasted almonds

Cook's Tip

If you're a chocoholic like me, you'll love this version of the Orange Almond Biscotti: Melt 8 ounces (225 g) of semisweet chocolate in a double boiler. Dip one side of the cooled biscotti into the chocolate and place on a wire rack for an hour to let the chocolate firm up.

Anise Twists

MAKES 32 COOKIES

These unusual twisted cookies make a striking addition to a dessert table. The speckles of anise seed give your tongue a burst of great licorice flavor. (Illustrated in this section.)

3 cups all-purpose flour

1 teaspoon baking powder

¼ teaspoon salt

2 teaspoons anise seed

1½ sticks (12 tablespoons) unsalted butter

1 cup sugar

2 eggs

1½ teaspoons vanilla extract

Combine the flour, baking powder, salt and anise seed in a medium bowl.

In a large bowl, beat the butter with an electric mixer until creamy. Add the sugar and beat until light and creamy. Beat in the eggs one at a time, then the vanilla. Stir in the dry ingredients. Gather the dough into a ball and flatten it into a thick disk. Wrap in plastic wrap and refrigerate for several hours or overnight.

Preheat the oven to 350° F (180° C). Grease 2 large baking sheets. Divide the dough into quarters, then cut each quarter into 8 pieces. Keep your hands lightly floured as you roll each piece into a 9-inch (23-cm) rope. Fold each rope in half and then twist it twice, pinching the ends together. Place the cookies 1-inch (2.5-cm) apart on the baking sheets. Bake for 12-15 minutes, until lightly browned. Transfer to wire racks to cool. The cookies will last for up to a week in a tightly sealed container.

Walnut Cake

Dense, nutty and lightly spiced with a honey-cinnamon syrup, this cake satisfies your sweet tooth without the extra calories of frosting. Make sure you use fresh nuts.

For the Vanilla Syrup, combine the sugar, water and honey in a medium saucepan. Bring to a boil over medium heat, stirring to dissolve the sugar. Add the cinnamon sticks or ground cinnamon and vanilla bean or vanilla extract, reduce the heat to low and simmer until thickened, about 10 minutes. Remove from the heat and cool.

For the Walnut Cake, preheat the oven to 350° F (180° C). Grease and flour a 9 x 13-inch (23 x 33-cm) cake pan. Sift together the flour, baking powder, ground cloves and salt. Set aside.

With an electric mixer, beat the butter and brown sugar in a large bowl, until creamy. Add the egg yolks, one at a time, beating well after each addition. Add the dry ingredients, mix well, then stir in the nuts and orange zest.

Clean the beaters carefully. In a clean bowl, beat the egg whites until stiff peaks form. Stir one-third of the beaten whites into the batter, then gently fold in the remaining whites. Pour the batter into the prepared cake pan and bake for 40 minutes, until the cake is golden brown and springs back when touched lightly with a finger. Remove from the oven.

Remove the cinnamon sticks and vanilla bean (if used) from the syrup and slowly pour it over the cake. It may seem as if there is too much syrup, but it will all be absorbed by the cake in about 10 minutes. Cut the cake into 18 squares and serve warm or at room temperature.

VANILLA SYRUP

½ cup sugar

¾ cup water

½ cup honey

2 (3-inch) (8-cm) cinnamon sticks or ½ teaspoon ground cinnamon

1 vanilla bean, split or 1 teaspoon vanilla extract

WALNUT CAKE

½ cup all-purpose flour

2 teaspoons baking powder

½ teaspoon ground cloves

¼ teaspoon salt

8 tablespoons (1 stick) unsalted butter, at room temperature

¼ cup brown sugar, packed

6 eggs, separated

2 cups ground walnuts

1 tablespoon grated orange zest

Chocolate Walnut Torte

SERVES 8 TO 10

This was a favorite during recipe testing. The walnuts not only provide a moist texture, they're the perfect contrast to the rich chocolate flavor. It's inspired from the chocolate cake that's served everywhere on the tiny resort island of Capri in the Bay of Naples.

6 ounces (175 g) unsweetened
   chocolate

8 tablespoons (1 stick)
   unsalted butter, at
   room temperature

1½ cups sugar

2 teaspoons vanilla

6 eggs, separated

1½ cups ground walnuts

½ cup all-purpose flour

¼ teaspoon salt

1 tablespoon powdered sugar

Preheat the oven to 350° F (180° C). Grease a 9-inch (23-cm) springform pan. Line the bottom with a circle of waxed paper cut to the diameter of the pan. Melt the chocolate in a small saucepan set on low heat, stirring until smooth. Set aside.

Beat the butter and ½ cup of the sugar in a large bowl, until light and creamy. Add the melted chocolate and vanilla, beating well. Add the egg yolks one at a time, beating well after each addition. Stir in the ground walnuts, flour and salt. The mixture will be moist but have a crumbly appearance.

Clean the beaters carefully. In a clean bowl, beat the egg whites until they are foamy. Gradually beat in the remaining sugar until stiff peaks form. Stir one-third of the beaten whites into the batter. Gently fold in the remaining whites.

Pour the batter into the prepared pan and smooth the top with a spatula. Bake for 50-60 minutes, until a toothpick inserted in the center comes out with some moist crumbs attached. Cool the cake in the pan for 10 minutes, then run a sharp knife around the edges to loosen the cake. Remove the pan sides and cool completely on a baking rack. Before serving, remove the waxed paper and transfer the cake to a serving platter. Sift the powdered sugar over the cake, cut into wedges and serve.

Love: A word properly applied to our delight
in particular kinds of food;
sometimes metaphorically spoken
of the favorite objects of all our appetites.

HENRY FIELDING (1707-1754)

FUNDAMENTALS

A Family That Cooks Together

You do not need to make everything from scratch to enjoy any one of my recipes. I will even go on record that, from time to time, I use canned tomato sauce, chicken stock or prepared pie dough. But you should know that I think it's the fundamentals - the stocks, roasted garlic, the sauces - that give these recipes the unique homemade taste that I remember from my childhood when my mother, grandmothers and aunts made everything from the fresh ingredients that were available.

When I was growing up, every day was market day for my Grandma Adele. She would often take me along on her trips by bicycle to the local farmers' market - a whole square block filled with tented stands where the farmers and traveling grocers sold their wares. With me tightly strapped into the child's seat in front of her, my little chubby legs (she called them *prosciuttini*, or "little prosciutti") dangling from the handlebars, we made our way through a bazaar of red tomatoes, yellow peppers and green zucchini, hanging prosciutti and soppressata salami, mounds of Parmigiano and baskets of fresh ricotta. I was not only introduced to the sights and smells of the food but to my grandma's own finely honed bargaining techniques. As she showed me how to judge the quality and freshness of the produce, I also learned a thing or two about negotiating which has helped me during my early career in business as much as it has in my life as a professional chef.

I loved being in the kitchen almost as much as I liked going to the market. Amidst the simmering pots of sauces, I would follow my assigned duties of shelling peas or peeling onions as the ceaseless chatter of my grandma, Aunt Buliti and my mom went on around me. It is only now that I have come to appreciate the culinary lessons I absorbed during those many hours.

As my Grandma Adele used to say, "A family that cooks together, stays together." And even though I am years and miles away from that familiar kitchen, with each dish I cook, I am carried back to those wonderful times.

Roasted Garlic

1 large head garlic

1 teaspoon olive oil

Slice the top one-third off the head of garlic, brush with the olive oil and place the sliced top back on. Wrap the garlic in aluminum foil and bake in a 400° F (200° C) oven for 35 minutes. When cool enough to handle, hold the head of garlic at the bottom and squeeze to force the pulp out. You can also remove individual cloves and squeeze them one at a time.

Onion Purée

Place all the ingredients in a 4-quart (3.75-l) stockpot. Bring to a boil, reduce the heat to medium and cook for 1 to 1½ hours, stirring every 15 minutes. Cook until all the liquid has evaporated and the onions have cooked down to a very thick consistency.

Remove the bay leaf. Put the onions in the food processor or blender and process until creamy. Place in ice cube trays and freeze. When frozen, take out of the trays and place in freezer bags.

The onion purée is used as a flavoring agent in other recipes.

Cook's Tip

This recipe will be very salty if you make it with regular canned stock. In order to avoid this, bring the canned stock to a boil, add 2 medium peeled and quartered potatoes and boil for 20 minutes. The potatoes will absorb much of the salt from the stock. Strain the stock and discard the potatoes. Don't add the salt called for in the recipe.

5 large onions, peeled and thinly sliced

1 bay leaf

1 teaspoon thyme

¼ teaspoon salt (see Cook's Tip)

¼ teaspoon pepper

1 cup dry Marsala wine

2 quarts (2 l) Chicken or Beef Stock (see pages 225 or 226)

Aioli

This garlicky mayonnaise from Provence goes with everything. Try it with bread, fish, chicken or vegetables, as is, or add puréed red peppers or chopped herbs as a flavor enhancement.

1 whole egg

1 egg yolk

¼ teaspoon salt

1 cup extra virgin olive oil

2 tablespoons lemon juice

6 garlic cloves, finely chopped
   (almost to a paste)

Process the egg, egg yolk and salt in a food processor or blender. With the motor still running, pour in half the olive oil in a very thin stream. Stop the motor and pour in the lemon juice. Turn the machine on again to blend the lemon juice, then continue adding the rest of the oil. Pour the oil faster as the aioli begins to thicken. When all the oil has been added, turn off the machine. Pour the aioli into a bowl and stir in the garlic. The aioli is ready to serve.

Cook's Tip

If you prefer a really garlicky sauce, add more garlic to taste.

Provençal Red Pepper Sauce

Known as rouille in Provence, this simple, colorful red pepper sauce is used to flavor fish soups. It's also great with other fish dishes, like Whole Fish Baked in a Salt Crust (page 141) or with vegetables. Try it on a baked potato!

Process the red peppers, garlic and egg yolk in a food processor or blender until smooth, about 1 minute. Add the salt, pepper, bread crumbs, Tabasco sauce, lemon juice, tomato paste, mustard and saffron or turmeric, if you wish. Process for 1 minute. Slowly add the olive oil in a thin stream. Transfer the sauce to a bowl and stir in the chopped parsley.

The sauce will keep for up to a week in the refrigerator in a covered container.

1 cup roasted red peppers, from a jar

3 garlic cloves

1 egg yolk

¼ teaspoon salt

⅛ teaspoon black pepper

3 tablespoons unseasoned bread crumbs

½ to 1 teaspoon Tabasco sauce (to taste)

2 tablespoons lemon juice

3 tablespoons tomato paste

1 tablespoon Dijon mustard

Pinch saffron powder or turmeric (optional)

⅓ cup extra virgin olive oil

¼ cup chopped fresh Italian parsley

Tomato Sauce

4 tablespoons olive oil

4 whole garlic cloves

¾ cup finely chopped onions

2 (28-ounce) (800-g) cans
    peeled Italian tomatoes

10 fresh basil leaves
    or 1 teaspoon dried

Pour the olive oil into a 3-quart (2.75-l) saucepan set on medium-high heat and cook the garlic and onion for 3-5 minutes. Reduce the heat to a simmer and cook until the onions are soft and begin to brown, about 10 minutes, stirring occasionally.

While the onions are cooking, put the tomatoes and their juices in a food processor or blender and process until smooth. Add the tomato purée to the onion mixture, raise the heat to high and bring to a boil for 5-8 minutes. Reduce the heat, add the basil and simmer for 25 minutes, stirring occasionally.

Cook's Tip

I can't stress enough the importance of using Italian tomatoes because they're naturally sweeter. If you have to use American tomatoes, double the amount of chopped onions and add 2 tablespoons of olive oil. Remember, this is a plain, unsalted sauce, which is great as an ingredient in other finished sauces. If you want to use this as a garnish for your pasta, I'd suggest you add ¼ teaspoon of salt for each 2 cups, according to your taste.

Vegetable Stock

Preheat the oven to 450° F (230° C). Place the onions, carrots, celery and garlic in a large bowl and toss with the olive oil. Place the vegetables on a baking sheet in a single layer and roast for 15 minutes. Remove the pan from the oven and toss the vegetables with the ketchup, until well coated. Return to the oven and cook for 15-20 minutes, until the ketchup has browned (caramelized) on the vegetables.

Put the vegetables in a large stockpot with the remaining ingredients. Bring to a boil, reduce the heat to low and simmer, uncovered, for 1 hour. Strain the stock through a fine sieve lined with cheesecloth. Let come to room temperature, then refrigerate.

The stock will keep up to 5 days refrigerated, or 1 month frozen.

2 onions, peeled and quartered

3 carrots, peeled and cut into thirds

4 stalks celery, cut into thirds

2 heads garlic cloves, unpeeled

2 tablespoons olive oil

¼ cup ketchup

3 whole cloves

½ teaspoon black peppercorns

1 bay leaf

4 sprigs parsley

5 quarts water

Shrimp Stock

2 tablespoons olive oil

Shells from 1 pound (450 g)
    shrimp

2 whole garlic cloves

1½ tablespoons chopped onion

1½ tablespoons chopped celery

1½ tablespoons chopped carrot

1 tablespoon tomato paste

1 tablespoon chopped fresh
    Italian parsley

1 teaspoon thyme

¼ cup white wine

4 cups clam juice

¼ teaspoon salt

¼ teaspoon black pepper

Cook the olive oil in a medium saucepan set on medium heat until sizzling, about 2 minutes. Add the shrimp shells, garlic, onion, celery, and carrot and cook for 5 minutes. Add the tomato paste, parsley, and thyme, increase the heat to high and cook for 2 minutes, stirring well. Add the wine and cook until it evaporates, about 3 minutes. Add the clam juice, bring to a boil and simmer, uncovered, for 30 minutes. Taste for salt and pepper.

Strain the stock through a fine sieve lined with cheesecloth. Let come to room temperature, then refrigerate.

The stock will keep up to 4 days refrigerated, or 1 month frozen.

Chicken Stock

⌄

MAKES 2 QUARTS (2L)

Place all the ingredients, including the egg shells, in a large stock pot and bring to a boil. Reduce the heat and simmer, with the cover slightly ajar, for 2 hours. Skim any foam that rises to the top every 30 minutes.

Remove the chicken and set aside to use in another recipe. Strain the stock through a fine sieve lined with cheesecloth. Place in the refrigerator until the next day. The fat will rise to the top, harden and become solid white. Skim it off and discard.

The stock will keep up to 4 days refrigerated, or 1 month frozen.

1 (3-pound) (1.4-kg) whole chicken, without the liver

2 small carrots, peeled and quartered

2 celery ribs, cut into 2-inch (5-cm) pieces

2 white onions, quartered

1 small fresh rosemary branch, about 4 inches (10 cm) or ½ teaspoon dried rosemary leaves

3 sprigs fresh Italian parsley

10 leaves fresh basil or 1 teaspoon dried

3 sprigs fresh thyme or ½ teaspoon dried

1 tablespoon black peppercorns

2 eggs, beaten well, egg shells reserved

1 cup white wine

¾ tablespoon salt

3¼ quarts (3.25 l) water

Beef Stock

5 pounds (2.4 kg) beef
   or veal bones, preferably
   shin bones

3 tablespoons tomato paste

1 tablespoon flour

1 large carrot, cut into 1-inch
   (2.5-cm) pieces

1 large onion, quartered

1 large celery rib, cut into
   1-inch (2.5-cm) pieces

1 teaspoon black peppercorns

5 whole cloves

2 bay leaves

2 sprigs fresh thyme or
   1½ teaspoons dried

5 sprigs fresh basil
   or ½ teaspoon dried

5 fresh sage leaves
   or ¼ teaspoon ground sage

2 sprigs fresh rosemary,
   about 3 inches (8 cm) each
   or 1 teaspoon dried leaves

1 gallon (3.75 l) water

Preheat the oven to 400° F (200° C). Place the bones in a large ovenproof pan and roast until well browned, turning twice, about 20-30 minutes. Remove from the oven.

In a large bowl, mix the tomato paste, flour, carrot, onion and celery. Spoon the mixture on top of the browned bones and roast in the oven for 15 minutes.

While the bones are cooking, make a cheesecloth pouch and place all the herbs and spices inside. Tie it securely with kitchen twine and put in a large stockpot.

Transfer the cooked vegetables and bones to the stockpot. Be careful not to pour in the fat that has accumulated in the bottom of the pan. Cover with the water and bring to a boil. Reduce the heat to a simmer and cook for 6-8 hours with the lid slightly ajar, without stirring. Check the water level. When you see that it is reduced by one-third (about half way through the simmering), add 3 cups of cold water.

Strain the stock, discarding the bones and vegetables. Let come to room temperature, then refrigerate overnight. The fat will rise to the top, harden and become solid white. Skim it off and discard.

The stock will keep up to 4 days refrigerated, or 1 month frozen.

Bolognese Meat Sauce

⌄

Heat the olive oil in a large saucepan set on high heat until sizzling, about 2 minutes. Add the red pepper flakes, celery, carrots, onion, garlic, bay leaf, sage, and basil and cook for 2 minutes, stirring constantly. Reduce the heat to medium-low and cook 10 minutes more, stirring occasionally. Raise the heat to high, add the prosciutto, veal, lamb and beef and cook, stirring constantly, for 2 minutes. Add the wine, reduce the heat to medium and let it cook until almost evaporated, about 5 minutes. Raise the heat to high, add the tomato sauce, tomato paste and stock and bring to a boil. Reduce the heat to a simmer, cover and cook for 45 minutes, stirring occasionally.

If you like your sauce thicker, remove the cover during the last 15 minutes of cooking. Add salt and pepper to taste.

5 tablespoons olive oil

¼ teaspoon red pepper flakes

½ cup finely chopped celery

½ cup finely chopped carrots

½ cup finely chopped onion

4 garlic cloves, thickly sliced

1 large bay leaf

1 tablespoon chopped fresh sage or ½ teaspoon ground

2 tablespoons chopped fresh basil or 2 teaspoons dried

2 ounces (60 g) finely diced prosciutto

¼ pound (115 g) ground veal

¼ pound (115 g) ground lamb

¼ pound (115 g) ground beef

⅓ cup red wine

½ cup Tomato Sauce (see page 222)

2 tablespoons tomato paste

2 cups Chicken or Beef Stock (see page 225 or 226)

Salt and pepper to taste

Béchamel Sauce

3 cups milk

3 tablespoons butter

3 tablespoons flour

⅛ teaspoon nutmeg

In a large saucepan set on medium heat, warm the milk until steaming. In another large saucepan, melt the butter over medium heat. Whisk the flour into the melted butter to form a thick paste or *roux*. Continue cooking for 2 minutes, stirring constantly. Do not let the flour brown. Remove the pan from the heat.

Add the nutmeg to the hot milk, then pour, a little at a time, into the warm roux, whisking vigorously to prevent lumps. When all the milk has been added, return the pan to medium heat and continue whisking until the sauce thickens, about 3-5 minutes. If the sauce is too thick, add a bit more milk; if it is too thin, cook a little longer. Remove from the heat, cover and set aside until ready to use.

You may prepare the sauce up to 2 hours ahead of time. Just rub the surface with a piece of butter to prevent a skin from forming and the sauce drying out.

Toasted Garlic Bread

Toast the bread slices under a broiler until the edges are brown on both sides, but the center is still white. Remove from the oven. When cool enough to handle, rub 1 side with a garlic clove.

Place the slices of garlic bread in an airtight container or self-sealing plastic bag until ready to use. The bread can be made up to 2 days ahead.

8 slices country-style Italian bread, sliced ½-¾ inch (1.5-2 cm) thick and halved

2-3 whole garlic cloves, peeled

Italian Bread Crumbs

½ teaspoon olive oil

1 cup plain bread crumbs

1 tablespoon finely chopped
   fresh basil
   or 1 teaspoon dried

1 tablespoon finely chopped
   fresh Italian parsley

⅛ teaspoon salt

⅛ teaspoon black pepper

2 tablespoons freshly grated
   Pecorino Romano
   or Parmigiano Reggiano
   cheese

Brush a nonstick sauté pan with the olive oil and cook over medium heat for 1 minute. Add the bread crumbs and cook, stirring, until brown, about 2 minutes.

Transfer to a bowl, add all the remaining ingredients and mix well. Store in an airtight container or self-sealing plastic bag. Leftover bread crumbs can be frozen up to 2 months.

Polenta

Bring the water and salt to a boil in a 3- to 4-quart (2.75- to 3.75-l) saucepan set on medium-high heat. Slowly whisk in the cornmeal. When all the cornmeal has been whisked in, begin stirring with a long-handled wooden spoon. (The polenta will spatter, so you might want to wear an oven mitt to protect yourself.) Reduce the heat to medium and stir continuously for 30-40 minutes, until the polenta is thick and comes away from the sides of the pan. Serve immediately.

4 cups water

1 teaspoon salt

1 cup cornmeal or imported polenta

Cook's Tip

A great variation on the basic polenta recipe is Grilled Polenta. To prepare, cook 1 recipe of polenta as directed above (or half of a 13-ounce (375-g) package of instant polenta), spread in a greased 9 x 9-inch (23 x 23-cm) baking pan and set aside for at least 30 minutes, until firm. Cut the polenta into 4 squares, then cut each square in half, from corner to corner, to make 2 triangles. Brush both sides of the cut polenta with 2 tablespoons of olive oil. Brush a little olive oil on the hot grill, as well. Grill each side for 4-5 minutes, 4-6 inches (10-15 cm) above medium-hot coals, until grill marks show and the polenta begins to brown.

For Broiled Polenta, place the polenta that has been brushed with 2 tablespoons of olive oil on a baking sheet. Position the broiler rack 4-6 inches (10-15 cm) from the heat source. Broil for 7-10 minutes, until lightly browned.

For Sautéed Polenta, heat the 2 tablespoons of olive oil in a large sauté pan set on high heat until sizzling, about 2 minutes. Place the triangles of polenta in the pan and cook for about 5 minutes on both sides, until golden brown.

Pie Dough

↓

MAKES 2 (8 OR 9-INCH) (20 OR 23-CM) TARTS OR 1 COVERED (8-INCH) (20-CM) TART

1¼ cups all-purpose flour

¼ teaspoon salt

2 tablespoons sugar

1 egg yolk

8 tablespoons (1 stick) cold unsalted butter, quartered lengthwise and cubed

3 tablespoons ice water

Place the flour, salt, sugar and egg yolk in a food processor fitted with a steel blade and pulse for 5 seconds to mix. Add the butter and pulse about 15 times, until the butter is the size of small peas. With the machine running, slowly add the water until the dough has formed a ball, about 10-15 seconds. Transfer the dough to a floured surface and knead lightly, about 1 minute. It is important not to over-knead the dough. When properly blended, the baked crust will be light and flaky.

To mix by hand, place the flour, salt and sugar in a bowl and stir to mix. Cut the butter into the flour mixture with a pastry blender or two knives, until the mixture resembles a coarse meal. With a fork, slowly stir in the egg yolk and then the ice water, mixing thoroughly. Transfer the dough to a lightly floured surface. Knead the dough briefly, until it comes together.

At this point, the dough may be patted into a tart pan. Chill for 30 minutes in the refrigerator. To use later, shape the dough into a flat disk, approximately 1 inch (2.5 cm) thick, wrap in plastic wrap and refrigerate for at least 45 minutes before rolling out to make the crust.

Unwrap the dough and divide in half for 2 (8-inch) (20-cm) tarts, or into two-thirds and one-third pieces for a covered tart. Place the dough for the bottom crust on a floured surface and roll out into a circle large enough to fit the pan. Ease the dough into the pan and trim the edges or form a decorative edge.

For a partially baked tart shell, prick the shell with a fork. Line the shell with aluminum foil, draping it over the edges. Fill with dried beans or pie weights. Bake in a preheated 375° F (190° C) oven for 15 minutes. Remove the foil and cool on a rack.

For a pre-baked shell, continue baking for 10 minutes longer, or until the shell is golden brown. Cool completely before filling.

Vegetarian Stuffing

MAKES 2 TO 2½ CUPS

Pour the olive oil into a nonstick sauté pan and cook the onion over medium-low heat until soft, about 3 minutes. Add the garlic and red pepper flakes and continue cooking for 5 minutes. Increase the heat to high, add the sliced mushrooms and the bay leaf and cook for 2 minutes, stirring well to prevent sticking.

Add the wine and cook until it has all evaporated, 3 more minutes. Stir in the chopped tomatoes, reduce the heat to medium and cook for 2 minutes. Add the parsley and the basil, stirring well. Pour in the reserved juice of the stewed tomatoes and cook over medium-low heat for 5 minutes, stirring occasionally. The mixture should be fairly thick and almost dry. If it is very watery, cook for 3 more minutes.

Transfer the mixture to a large mixing bowl. Add the egg, bread crumbs and cheese and mix well. The stuffing should be very thick and fairly moist. If it is still watery, add more cheese and bread crumbs.

2 tablespoons olive oil

½ red onion, finely chopped

4 garlic cloves, thickly sliced

⅛ teaspoon red pepper flakes

¾ pound (350 g) white button mushrooms, sliced

1 bay leaf

¾ cup white wine

1 (14½-ounce) (415-g) can stewed tomatoes, drained and chopped, juices reserved separately

1 tablespoon chopped fresh Italian parsley

1 tablespoon chopped fresh basil

1 large egg

¾ cup Italian Bread Crumbs (see page 230)

½ cup freshly grated Pecorino Romano cheese

Gnocchi
    fisherman's, 93
    with creamy asparagus-prosciutto sauce, 92

Gorgonzola pork chops, 124

Greek salad, 59

Greek salad with tuna, 60

Green beans,
    oven roasted vegetables, 152

Grilled polenta with mushroom sauce, 109

H

Hazelnut
    shortbread, crunchy, 206

Honey
    orange mousse with raspberries, 187
    vanilla rice flan, 194

Hummus bi tahini, 13

I

Italian
    bread crumbs, 230
    meat pockets, 129
    mocha cream pudding, 189

L

Lamb
    and lentil soup, 52
    Bolognese meat sauce, 227
    rack of, with mustard, garlic and
        rosemary, 134-135

Turkish kebabs, 136-137

Lasagne
    spinach, 83
    with Bolognese meat sauce, 90

Leek(s)
    and artichoke sauce, pasta with, 80

Lemon
    pistachio cream, frozen, 191
    soufflé, 195

Lentil(s)
    and lamb soup, 52
    salad, French, 62
    soup, French, 53

M

Main courses
    asparagus frittata, 108
    baked fish fillets, 142
    beef and bell pepper stew, 130
    braised beef and olives, 131
    chicken cordon bleu, 116
    chicken scallopini with ham and
        asparagus, 117
    chicken with garlic sauce, 114-115
    eggplant Parmesan, 110
    French pepper steaks, 128
    ginger tuna, 140
    Gorgonzola pork chops, 124
    grilled polenta with mushroom sauce, 109
    Italian meat pockets, 129
    Mediterranean shepherd's pie, 132-133
    Moroccan chicken and almond pie, 122-123
    Moroccan chicken with olives, 120

N

O

T

Tomatoes, sun-dried
and cheese spread on garlic toast, 16
pasta with pine nuts and, 75

Tuna (canned)
and white bean spread on garlic toast, 20
chickpea salad and, 63
Greek salad with, 60
pasta with asparagus and, 95

Tuna (fresh)
with ginger, 140

Tunisian
chickpea soup, 50
stewed potatoes, 25

Turkey
scallopini with curry sauce, 121

Turkish kebabs, 136-137

Twice-baked spinach potatoes, 162

V

Vegetable(s). *See also* Appetizers; Entrées;
Side dishes; Soups and salads
oven roasted, 152
Provençal baked, 153
stock, 223

Vegetarian Stuffing, 233

W

Walnut cake, 209

Wild mushroom soup, 43

Whole fish baked in a salt crust, 141

Z

Zabaglione
chocolate, 184
espresso, 183

Zucchini
cannelloni with prosciutto and, 88
pasta with eggplant, tomatoes and, 76
pasta with shrimp and, 94
Provençal baked vegetables, 153
ratatouille, 23

Carissimi amici, (Dear friends,)
Thank you for choosing my Mediterranean Flavors cook-book, the third in the Cucina Amore series. I hope you enjoy the recipes, and that you will let me know if you have any comments or questions. If you would like to hear about new Cucina Amore products and special appearances, please fill out the coupon below.
Grazie e arrivederci,
Nick Stellino
Cucina Amore

Non ti scordar di me! (Don't forget me!)

I WANT TO DISCOVER MORE NEW IDEAS FROM CUCINA AMORE!

MY NAME

ADDRESS

CITY   STATE / ZIP

PHONE NUMBER (OPTIONAL) (   )
AREA CODE

DETACH & MAIL TO:
CUCINA AMORE, DEPT. 203, P.O. BOX 84848, SEATTLE, WA 98124

CUCINA AMORE